The Gospel Miracles:
What Really Happened?

The Gospel Miracles:
What Really Happened?

A Systematic, Open-Minded Review
of the Evidence

Michael J. Lowis

Foreword by
Alan Jeffrey Taylor

RESOURCE *Publications* · Eugene, Oregon

THE GOSPEL MIRACLES: WHAT REALLY HAPPENED?
A Systematic, Open-Minded Review of the Evidence

Resource Publications
An Imprint of Wipf and Stock Publishers
199 W. 8th Ave., Suite 3
Eugene, OR 97401

www.wipfandstock.com

ISBN 13: 978-1-4982-0427-9

Manufactured in the U.S.A.   10/27/2014

CONTENTS

TABLES AND FIGURE

FOREWORD

I HAVE KNOWN DR Mike Lowis for a great many years, and have followed his career with interest. He has published academic articles on an impressive range of topics, including the psychology of humour, life satisfaction in older adults, the emotional effect of music and, more recently, on spiritual and religious matters. When he invited me to copy-edit his most recent work on the Gospel miracles, I was happy to accept the challenge, although I was not sure what to expect.

On reading his manuscript, it is clear that the investigation has involved him in a very careful analysis of the relevant biblical texts, a painstaking and honest evaluation of the evidence for events that took place two thousand years ago, and a consideration of present-day medical and psychological knowledge.

In the end, Mike has arrived at what he hopes will be seen as an unbiased, if unashamedly theist, interpretation of the miracles. This may not meet with universal approval but I myself, an agnostic in such matters, found the book refreshing and informative. I would certainly recommend it to readers of faith, and of no faith, who wish to improve their knowledge of the New Testament and the ideas expressed in it.

Jeff Taylor

Bingley
United Kingdom

PREFACE

WHEN I FIRST CONTEMPLATED undertaking this investigation into what really happened with the Gospel miracles, I had some genuine reservations. My early training and experience was in laboratory work, specializing in microbiology. This can be regarded as one of the 'hard' sciences, where manipulation of the elements involved in its practice can be relied upon to inevitably yield predictable outcomes. Later I changed to the social sciences and ultimately obtained a doctorate in psychology. Whilst this 'soft' science does not yield experimental outcomes as predictably certain as do those in the hard sciences, the results from a well-conducted and controlled study are often reliable to a level of ninety-five percent or greater.

In both these careers I concentrated on research wherever possible, and delighted in publishing results that demonstrated new methodologies or yielded novel predictions or relationships between different variables. For the third stage of my career I embarked on a study of theology, which is still in progress at the time of writing. Not only is some experiential or research work an important part of any university degree course, including theology, this aspect has continued to be a major interest in my academic journey. Although several of my psychology research studies have embraced religion and spirituality, including how people came to have their faith and in what ways does it support them, I have until recently held back on a major study that involves a rational investigation of biblical narratives.

I asked myself if it would be inappropriate to try and apply scientific methodology to events described in the Scriptures. Many regard the biblical texts as either God given or at least God inspired, and that they must therefore be regarded as inerrant. In other words, if the Bible states that Jesus went somewhere, did something or spoke certain words, then this should be taken as fact and not questioned. On the other hand, the texts were penned about 2,000 years ago, probably from memory and sometimes from second-hand sources. Added to this, no original manuscripts have survived, and the words we read today have been copied and translated many times, with opportunities for error at every stage. If we compound this with the fact that the writers were living in a very different culture and situation than readers are today, and that they did not have our current level of scientific knowledge, the chances of misunderstanding or misreporting are surely real. The attempt to unravel all this and reveal the true meaning is the task of exegesis, and even skilled and experienced exegetes can fail to agree.

Eventually I could not resist the urge to embark on a research study of my own, and I chose a topic of particular interest to me, namely: to investigate what really happened with the Gospel miracles and whether or not they can they be explained rationally. I would like to emphasize most strongly that this was certainly *not* an attempt to disprove or deny any of the miracles, or detract from their importance and relevance at the time they were performed, or indeed the meaning they have for many people today. The attempted explanations were conducted with an open mind as possible, and the investigation followed a methodology that combined sound exegetical principles with a procedure I developed earlier to investigate topics not suitable for study using the orthodox scientific method.

I hope the reader will find the investigation and the outcomes of interest. They are free to reject them completely as inappropriate, or to accept that they may shed some light on what actually occurred. Any suggestion of a rational explanation does not in any way remove the possibility that were enacted using the natural laws in opportune ways, rather than overriding them. I ask the reader to forgive me if I have transgressed what he or she regards as an inappropriate examination of the accounts of miracles that appear in the Bible, or that I may have arrived at conclusions with which the reader strongly disagrees. At all times the study was conducted with an unbiased and open-minded approach as possible, with the sole aim of trying to establish what actually occurred.

Michael J. Lowis

Northampton
United Kingdom

ACKNOWLEDGEMENTS

I WISH TO THANK A. J. ("Jeff") Taylor for his detailed and systematic copy-editing of this manuscript; he pointed out many errors, inaccuracies and grammatical lapses caused by over familiarity with the text, and he made useful suggestions to improve consistency.

I also am very grateful to Dr David Major who provided invaluable advice on the medical aspects of some of the healing miracles, and also checked and corrected my transliterations from the Greek texts.

My thanks are also extended to artist Elizabeth Davies who created the illustrations for this book.

INTRODUCTION

THE PURPOSE OF THIS book is to report the outcome of a study on the accounts that appear in the four New Testament Gospels of miracles performed by Jesus. It will inter alia include discussions on the definition, accuracy of reporting, purpose, expectations, and explanations of these events. Reports of miracles are, however, not restricted to the Gospels. There are about seventy-five such examples in the Old Testament (OT), most being either in the Moses narratives of Exodus and Numbers, for example the parting of the Red Sea (Exod 14: 21), and the Elijah/Elisha narratives in 1 and 2 Kings, including the widow's son being raised from the dead (1 Kgs 17:22) (Moberly, 2011)[1].

As will be discussed in the main body of this report with regard to the works of Jesus, opinion is sometimes divided on just what should be included in the list. In the OT, for example, the creation of the universe as reported in Genesis was surely an act of God, but should it be classified as a miracle? Likewise, were the plagues of Egypt such as those of frogs, lice and flies, as reported in Exodus, or the hailstorm that killed the Amorites as written in Joshua 10:11, miraculous events or just natural albeit extreme phenomena?

In the New Testament (NT), miracles are cited in books other than the four Gospels. In addition to providing specific examples, the book of Acts states: "The apostles performed many signs and wonders among the people" (5:12, this and all subsequent

---

1. *Miracles in the Hebrew Bible*, 62–63.

quotations are taken from the New International Version of the Bible [NIV] unless otherwise stated), and "God did extraordinary miracles through Paul" (19:11). Paul himself writes about spiritual gifts and he notes: "to another [is given] gifts of healing" (1 Cor 12:10) and, concerning himself: "I persevered in demonstrating among you the marks of a true apostle, including signs, wonders and miracles" (2 Cor 12:12). The Gospels also record events that applied to Jesus himself, most importantly his virgin birth, transfiguration, and resurrection, each of which provides abundant scope for discussion, but the present investigation will instead be restricted to the miracles carried out *by* Jesus.

Reports of miracles are not restricted to the Bible but also appear in non-biblical texts, but belief in miraculous events and written accounts of them are widespread in antiquity (Keener, 2011)[2]. Among the many pagan examples of miracle workers are the Egyptian deities Serapis and Isis, with the latter being credited with not only healing powers but also the ability to rescue people from prison and protect them at sea (Garland, 2011)[3]. One of the most prominent superhuman healers in ancient Greece was Asclepius, son of Apollo. Shrines to this deity were popular from about the fourth century BC, and were often situated near healthy springs to which people flocked for healing. In the first century AD Vespasian, before he became emperor, was reported to have cured a blind man with his spittle, and the pagan philosopher Apollonius of Tyana was reputed to have miraculous healing powers. However, as Trench (1850)[4] states, unlike the miracles of Jesus, those of the pagan healers did not serve a higher purpose.

Pre-Christian Jewish reports of miracles are evidenced firstly by OT accounts, often associated with dramatic events such as freak weather, fires, floods, and plagues but also with occasional healings and raisings from the dead. An example from non-biblical rabbinical literature relates to Honi HaM'agel who drew a circle, stepped into it and successfully prayed for rain (Novakovic,

2. *Ancient Miracle Claims Outside Christianity*, 35–82.
3. *Miracles in the Greek and Roman World*, 75–94.
4. *Notes on the Miracles of our Lord*, 60–63.

2011)[5]. Jewish healers were also known at the time of Jesus and later. Among those cited by first-century Romano-Jewish scholar and historian Josephus was Eleazar, who practiced exorcism. The Talmud also mentions the charismatic healer and miracle worker Hanina ben Dosa.

Despite the widespread reports of miracles in ancient times, and many modern claims (vide infra), the present study will be restricted to those carried out by Jesus, as cited in the four Gospels. Whilst in any research it is always difficult to remain unbiased, the present writer will nevertheless attempt to maintain an open mind, avoiding over-reliance on scientific rationalism on the one hand, and an uncritical 'leap of faith' acceptance of biblical inerrancy on the other. However, although retaining a theist world view the writer, for this investigation will, of necessity, adopt a liberal rather than conservative position, otherwise no questioning of the biblical reports could be undertaken. For the sake of guidance, therefore, the following hypothesis will be explored: *all the reported miracles of Jesus are amenable to rational explanation.* Like all hypotheses, this one is capable of falsification (Popper, in Speake, 1979)[6].

Where appropriate the "supported philosophical-deductive approach", devised earlier by the writer for investigating topics not amenable to investigation by conventional scientific methodology (Lowis, 2004)[7], will be used. This involves seeking evidence to corroborate or refute the "alternative" premise in a series of deductive arguments. In the present study, the premise will be that a particular miracle was the result of a divine intervention not amenable to rational explanation and which must, therefore, be accepted by faith alone. The alternative, for which evidence will be sought, will be that there is a rational explanation for the event. If the alternate is not supported then the original premise stands, not because it has been *proved* but because it has survived attempts to *disprove* it. The more attempts the premise survives, on weight of evidence the more chance there is that it is true. Of course, the likelihood of a

---

5. *Miracles in the Second Temple and Early Rabbinic Judaism*, 95–112.

6. *Popper*, 262–63.

7. *A Novel Method to Study the Propensity to Appreciate Music*, 105–11.

naturalistic explanation does not rule out the possibility, or even the probability, that Jesus employed nature at the right time and place to achieve His objectives.

Finally, whilst this will be a rational exercise, Barth's (1949)[8] statement that "In the miracles of Jesus there is triumph and joy" will be kept in mind throughout the process.

8. *Dogmatics in Outline*, 102.

CHAPTER 1

WHAT IS A MIRACLE?

ALTHOUGH THE TERM "MIRACLE" is common terminology for a range of apparently supernatural events cited in the Scriptures and elsewhere, including in modern reports, it is not the most frequently used term for this in the Bible. "Signs", "wonders", "works", and "powers" are among the other descriptions (Butler, 2001)[1].

Olander (2006)[2] explains that there are differences and nuances that must be considered in the use of these alternative expressions. For example, "miracle" is a common biblical interpretation of the Greek *dunamis*, which literally means "power", "might" or "strength" (Note: all Koine translations are taken from Friberg et al., *Lexicon*, 2005). Likewise *Semeion* is translated as "sign" or "distinguishing mark", *teras* as "wonder", "marvel", or "portent", whilst *ergon* is "work", "deed", or "action". There are just nine uses of the term "miracles" in the NIV version of the Synoptic Gospels, for example "What are these remarkable miracles he is performing?" (Mark 6:2), but none in John. The fourth Gospel does, however, contain eight mentions of "signs" ("many people saw the signs he was performing." John 2:23) compared with just two in Matthew and one in Mark. "Wonders" (a word that suggests an audience reaction: Moberly, 2011)[3] appears for example in Acts "I will show

1. *Holman Concise Bible Dictionary*, 431.
2. *Signs, Miracles and Wonders*, 41.
3. *Miracles in the Hebrew Bible*, 57–74.

wonders in the heavens above" (2:19), along with "works" "What must we do to do the works God requires?" (John 6:28).

The Chambers Dictionary (2001)[4] defines a miracle as "An event or act which breaks a law of nature, especially one attributed to a deity or supernatural force." From a theological standpoint this definition is inadequate and the reference to breaking a law of nature is simplistic, although Montefiore (2005)[5] in similar vein refers to events that violate the accepted order of nature, or are statistically exceedingly improbable even if possible. Butler's (2001)[6] offering is quite specific regarding divine intervention: "Events that unmistakably involve an immediate and powerful action of God designed to reveal his character or purpose". He also notes that the Bible makes no clear-cut distinction between the "natural" (God working providentially) and the "supernatural" (God working in striking ways), an observation that will be revisited vide infra. Blackburn (1992)[7] is likewise unambiguous in stating that miracles are supernatural events that transcend ordinary happenings, due to the exercise of God's power either directly or through human or superhuman agents.

Others scholars are somewhat more circumspect by suggesting that the beholders need to evaluate what they have witnessed. For example, Eichhorst (1968)[8] suggests: "an extraordinary event inexplicable in terms of ordinary natural forces . . . which causes the observer to postulate a superhuman personal cause." Similarly, Basinger (2011)[9] defines miracles as "unusual, remarkable events that it is assumed would not have occurred in the context in question if not for the intentional activity of a benevolent supernatural being." Larmer (2011)[10] likewise emphasizes events that would not have otherwise occurred, adding that they are seen as interventions

---

4. *Miracle*, 1026.

5. *The Miraculous, the Mythical and the Paranormal*, 2.

6. *Holman Concise Bible Dictionary*, 431.

7. *Miracles and Miracle Stories*, 549.

8. *The Gospel Miracles—Their Nature and Apologetic Values*, 12.

9. *What is a Miracle?*, 19.

10. *The Meaning of Miracles*, 36.

of the normal order of nature, whilst Levine (2011)[11] quotes Aquinas as stating that they are divine interventions beyond the order commonly observed in nature.

Thus the majority view is that, in the first instance, a miracle is an occurrence that strikes the witness as unusual, either because of the time and the place of its occurrence, or the fact that no natural explanation for its cause is forthcoming. This is not to say that a naturalistic explanation is impossible but that, if one exists, it is beyond the witness's current level of knowledge or understanding. Following on from this, the witness needs to draw some sort of conclusion that is satisfying for him or her, and therefore avoids the cognitive dissonance that would occur if there were no explanation. A theist might well conclude that the event was an act of God, in other words a divine miracle, whilst an atheist could say that either it was a case of trickery or that there is a naturalistic explanation waiting to be discovered, even if this may be some way in the future.

Because most commentators link their definitions with a non-natural causality, it is necessary to consider just what is a "law of nature". Whilst many would assume such laws are by definition fixed and inviolable, Trench (1850)[12] states that they exist only for us, not for God who acts on his will: miracles may be beyond and above nature but not contrary to it. Similarly, Wright (1927)[13] regards the laws as infinite in extent and thus a miracle does not violate them as such. The view that "laws of nature" are not necessarily sacrosanct is supported by the notion that these laws never actually *cause* an event, but are formulated to describe observations—they are not prescriptive (Keener, 2011[14]; Larmer, 2011[15]), although of course it should be added that their predictions are invariably reliable. As Basinger (2011)[16] notes, laws dictate what

11. *Philosophers on Miracles*, 291.

12. *Notes on the Miracles of Our Lord*, 15.

13. *Miracles*, 186-91.

14. *Hume and the Philosophical Questions*, 135–6.

15. *The Meaning of Miracles*, 38.

16. *What is a miracle?*, 24-5.

happens under specified conditions, but science is continually discovering new information on causal relationships. This leaves open the possibility of a future natural explanation for events that currently defy a rational explanation.

Erickson (1985)[17] opines that miracles do seem to defy science's picture of the regularity of the universe, but he pertinently adds that modern science relies on statistical probability for its laws, not certainty. He notes that there are three possible ways that miracles relate to nature: they are either manifestations of virtually unknown natural laws, they break the laws of nature, or they are caused by supernatural forces. Larson (2003)[18], however, states that there are just two possibilities: God either works *without* the laws of nature (for example when changing water into wine) or he works *against* them (for example when raising people from the dead), but Larson somewhat ambiguously concludes that God will *not violate* these laws. Twelftree (2011)[19] also does not consider that miracles violate the laws of nature, as he states that God either directly manipulates the natural order or that he predetermines that nature will bring about miraculous events. He adds that a miracle remains as such even if a natural explanation is forthcoming.

In reviewing these diverse opinions, it is intuitively easier to accept that miracles do not blatantly violate the known laws of nature, but either providentially make use of them or comply with laws yet to be discovered, than it is to maintain that God can and does completely violate the laws when the need arises. Whilst this is the writer's conclusion, it must inevitably remain just a viewpoint as the ultimate truth is likely to remain elusive and will be influenced by the beholder's personal faith.

17. *Providence and Miracles*, 406–9.

18. *Three Centuries of Objections to Biblical Miracles*, 78-79.

19. *Introduction: Miracle in an Age of Diversity*, 3.

CHAPTER 2

RELIABILITY OF THE BIBLICAL ACCOUNTS

BEFORE ATTEMPTING TO INTERPRET and explain miracles, it is pertinent to first consider factors that might affect the accuracy of the biblical accounts of them. If there is doubt about the historical reporting, then it will be necessary to try and deduce what really happened before attempting an explanation.

The events described in the OT are estimated to commence from about 2,000 BC when Abraham was believed to have entered Canaan, but it is unlikely that these stories were written down until at least five hundred years later. The first five books—the Pentateuch, also known as the Torah—are held by many to have been written by Moses around 1405 to 1445 BC, with the earlier events having being preserved and passed down through oral tradition. None of the original writings remain today, but the Hebrew texts were translated into Greek in about 250 BC and are referred to as the Septuagint (LXX). In an attempt to obtain a standard text, Jewish scholars—the Masorites, working from the ninth to the fifteenth century—compared all known manuscripts and produced what is known as the Masoretic Text (MT). After such a long process of oral tradition, translations, copying and with no doubt a degree of editing at each stage, discretion may be needed when assessing the historical accuracy of at least some of the OT miracle reports.

Similar reservations apply to NT accounts, even though they were penned much later than those in the OT. The Gospels were mostly written in Greek during the first century AD, in the Middle-eastern world of Judaism, when Judah was part of the Roman Empire. As with the Hebrew texts, no original manuscripts have survived, and what is contained in the Bible, especially in modern translations, has been copied, translated and edited many times over the last two thousand years. Whilst the time lag is less than for the Pentateuch, it is unlikely that any of the original texts were written down at the time of the happenings they describe, but were probably passed on by oral tradition or retained in the memories of the witnesses for thirty years or more before they were documented.

Like all writings, regardless of claims of objectivity, the Gospels were written from a personal point of view, during a particular time and in particular circumstances or *Sitz im Leben*. Thus the task of establishing the true facts, let alone the intended meaning, of any of the biblical accounts remains a challenging task for exegetical scholars and interpreters, including the present writer in his examination of the miracle narratives. Even then, just as the Gospel writers wrote from their own viewpoints, today's interpreters sometimes struggle to avoid being influenced by their own presuppositions and biases. This makes the task of trying to understand and explain the miracles objectively neither a straight forward nor a simple one. Throughout history scholars have see-sawed between a largely allegorical interpretation of the Scriptures, as practiced for example by the Alexandrian patristic school, and a more plain and literal understanding as favored by the school at Antioch (Bray, 1996)[1].

Moderate Christians would no doubt accept the Scriptures as God inspired, but may hesitate to claim that they are inerrant. However, they would also tend to avoid the strong liberal view that everything that is written is subjective and can be interpreted virtually as one wishes. An anonymous writer in *Bibliotheca Sacra* (1914)[2] examined the reliability of biblical evidence based on the

1. *Patristic Interpretation*, 77–89.
2. *"Studies in Theology"* and Hume's *"Essay on Miracles"*, 105-31.

principles of jurisprudence, the science that deals with the competency of what is proposed as evidence. The writer concluded that the Bible can be legally regarded as a properly preserved 'ancient document', and therefore the eyewitness reports, being accurately recorded, are admissible as evidence. According to Kelly (2008)[3], the reliability of the miracle reports is further supported by the fact that there were often many witnesses to these events. Additionally, over 50 percent of them are recorded in more than one Gospel, with the authors drawing, to a greater or lesser extent, on independent sources. Whilst the evidence does not constitute scientific proof, it is sufficient to challenge the honest enquirer (Blackburn, 1992)[4]. As Marshall (2004)[5] concluded, we may regard the Bible as 'infallible' rather than 'inerrant', and should apply diligent study to uncover the original meaning and what it means to us today.

There are, however, other considerations that are pertinent to reports of miracles. Especially with the time lapse between the events themselves and the penning of the first accounts, there is the problem of reliability of memory. The term 'flash bulb memory' has been coined to describe the vivid images of a dramatic event confidentially recalled by witnesses where evidence has subsequently shown that some of the details of such memories have been forgotten. Research on eyewitness testimony, notably by Elizabeth Loftus, has generated some surprising results. For example, a study involving mock court cases showed that, regardless of the true facts, witnesses who gave the most detailed accounts, including of trivial aspects, were considered to be more reliable than those who gave less detail (Bell & Loftus, 1988)[6]. A later study revealed that the memory of real traumatic events can be experimentally contaminated: on two occasions separated by six months, students were asked to recall details of the attacks on

3. *Miracle, Method, and Metaphysics,* 45–66.

4. *Miracles and Miracle Stories,* 549–60.

5. *What are the Results of Inspiration?,* 72–73.

6. *Degree of Detail of Eyewitness Testimony and Mock Juror Judgements,* 1171–92.

Moscow apartment buildings. During the intervening period, false suggestions were made to the participants that they had included in their first reports a mention of a wounded animal. A significant number of the students duly supplied details of this in their second reports, even adding additional details of their own (Nourkove, Bernstein & Loftus, 2004)[7].

Dreams can also help to confuse the issue of what is fact or fiction, and it is a common belief that they may contain hidden truths or predict future events. Biblical examples include Joseph's interpretation of Pharaoh's dream (Gen 41:138) and Daniel's interpretation of Nebuchadnezzar's dream (Dan 4:19-35). Careful investigation of more modern examples, however, casts doubt on the belief that the images and messages of dreams originate from outside sources (Lowis, 2010)[8]. So important do some people regard dreams that their interpretations of them can impact on their everyday lives (Morewedge et al., 2009)[9]. Although they tend to endorse pre-existing beliefs, including faith in God, people sometimes believe that what they dreamt about had actually happened. When we are asleep and dreaming there are several neurological changes, one of which is that the part of the brain responsible for voluntary movement is largely inoperative so the body is paralyzed. This effect normally decreases as we awaken but, if we wake up suddenly, some paralysis can remain along with hallucinations (Lowis, 2010)[10]. False memories can also be formed so that we are convinced that events depicted in our dreams actually did happen. Among other things, this is believed to be the origin of a belief that one has been abducted by aliens.

The purpose of the above review is not to claim that biblical accounts of miracles are necessarily erroneous, but to indicate that factors such as long delays before recording in writing, inaccurate recall, presuppositions of the observer, eyewitness errors, false

---

7. *Altering Traumatic Memory*, 575–85.

8. *Dreams and their relation to Physical and Mental Well-being*, 366–80.

9. *When Dreaming is Believing*, 249–64.

10. *Dreams and their relation to Physical and Mental Well-being*, 366-80.

memories, and the possible intermixing of dreams with reality may all have affected the reliability and accuracy of what we read today.

There have always been people who completely deny the credibility of miracles, and Trench (1850)[11] reviews the history of such groups or individuals, commencing with Jews in Jesus' time who believed that such events were trickery or the work of the devil. For example "The Pharisees . . . said 'it is only by Beelzebul, the prince of demons, that this fellow drives out demons'" (Matt 12:24). The heathens had their own healers (e.g. Asclepius, vide supra), whilst the Pantheists (e.g. Spinoza, 1632 to 1677) thought that God would be contradicting himself if he broke his own laws. German theologian and philosopher Schleiermacher (1768 to 1834) thought that miracles were only for those who first witnessed them, as the means for them already resided in nature and just needed evoking, whilst rationalists such as Paulus (1761 to 1851) held that there were simple, naturalistic explanations such as that new wine had been brought into the wedding feast (see vide infra, the water into wine miracle, John 2:1–11).

Perhaps the most notorious proponent of the skeptical view of miracles is Scottish philosopher and historian David Hume (1711 to 1776). His basic premise was that, because of the unreliability of eyewitness testimony in religious cases, and the physical impossibility of overriding a descriptive law of nature, the historian is committed to dismissing cases for the miraculous as 'not proven' (Speake, 1979)[12]. Both the reliability of biblical evidence and the laws of nature were discussed earlier in the present report, and the data therein suggest that Hume's assumptions may be flawed. He bases his conclusions with regard to the natural laws on a blind acceptance that they are forever inviolable and, unlike the anonymous writer in *Bibliotheca Sacra* (1914), he discounts out of hand the reliability of the eyewitness testimony.

What Hume stated in his 1748 *Essay on miracles* (in Watson, 1990)[13] was that the miracle stories rely on testimony that

11. *The Assults on Miracles*, 57–85.

12. *Hume*, 142–46.

13. *Enlightenment*, 191–94.

contradicts our usual experience: there is not enough past experience to warrant belief in a miracle. He concludes that no testimony is sufficient to establish a miracle unless its falsehood would be more miraculous than the event it endeavors to establish. Whilst Hume fell short of stating that miracles were not theoretically possible, he maintained that no evidence to date had shown that the uniformity of nature has been violated (Montefiore, 2005)[14]. He continued that, if this were the case, how then are the reports to be explained? Hume states that the only answer is to claim that they were never intended to be taken as literally true, but were told to disclose the meaning of Jesus' ministry (this symbolic view is included in the next section of this report: 'Suggested explanations of Jesus' miracles').

Whilst Hume extolled the improbability of miracles based on the pertaining Enlightenment philosophy and its faith in scientific rationalism, Larmer (2011)[15] reverses this probability argument by stating "If affirming the existence of God would render an event more comprehensible than otherwise, then the event is independent evidence that God exists." He concludes that, on scientific and theological grounds, belief in miracles is entirely rational. This concurs with the view of Kelly (2008)[16] that a major problem with the acceptance of miracles is the existence of a prejudicial bias against them. If this can be swept away then the evidence can be considered on its merits alone. He concludes that a good case can be made for a personal and powerful God, and that there is an "intrinsic probability" concerning certain (miraculous) events.

Thus it is evident that Hume's objections to miraculous claims are based on a closed-minded circular argument, namely that miracles violate the laws of nature that have been established by experience, whilst denying the possibility that new experiences and the credible accounts of witnesses can lead to new laws, or a better understanding of existing ones (Keener, 2011)[17].

14. *The Miraculous, The Mythical and the Paranormal*, 1-8.

15. *The Meaning of Miracles*, 47

16. *Miracle, Method, and Metaphysics: Philosophy and the Quest for the Historical Jesus*, 45–66.

17. *Hume's Epistemology Regarding Miracles*, 143–47.

CHAPTER 3
EYE WITNESS EXPECTIONS

INEVITABLY, DESPITE ILLUSIONS OF independence, most of us are influenced in our thinking and attitudes by the social milieu that surrounds us and the pertaining cultural beliefs, and no doubt this also applied to those who lived at the time of Jesus.

As Ropes (1910)[1] observed over a century ago, in ancient times the view that people had of the world was more simplistic than the one we have today with our knowledge of science and technology. The belief that events in the physical world can be explained rationally in terms of processes in this world is barely two centuries old, and is radically different from the beliefs of early Christians (Wells, 2010)[2]. The pious Israelites saw God as the source of all activity, with his hand being present in nature. Miracles were held to belong to the natural concept of God's working, and were accepted as such. Even in NT times witnesses would have seen healings and some other events as miraculous for which today we might have rational explanations. Starting with a hint in Genesis 3:15 ("I will put enmity between . . . your offspring and hers [Eve's] and he will crush your head"), and continuing throughout the OT, there is an anticipation of the coming of a Messiah and the progressive revelation of his character (Deffinbaugh, 2004)[3].

1. *Some Aspects of New Testament Miracles*, 482–99.

2. *Miracles and the New Testament*, 43–59.

3. *https://bible.org/article/anticipation-israels-messiah*

The Israelites were looking forward to the arrival of such a savior; this hope and anticipation was the basis of the believer's faith and provided substance for his or her conduct and worship.

Blackburn (1992)[4] notes that Jesus was regarded by many at that time as this predicted Mosaic prophet: "The Lord your God will raise up for you a prophet like me from among you" (Deut 18:15), a statement quoted by both Peter and Stephen as recorded in Acts (3:23 and 7:37 respectively). The witnesses would thus have not been surprised by the wondrous acts performed by Jesus, because they regarded miracles as legitimate acts when carried out by divinely appointed agents. As noted by Wells (2010)[5], the early Christians expected God to intervene in the world in wonderful ways. The signs, wonders and miracles enacted by Jesus thus served to confirm the message and that he was indeed the messenger (Olander, 2006)[6]. This was recognized by Nicodemus, among others, when he is reported to have said to Jesus: " . . . we know you are a teacher who has come from God. For no one could perform the signs you are doing if God were not with him." (John 3:2).

Another possible influencing factor, only recently identified, might also have pertained at the time of Jesus. Lerner and Miller (1978)[7] formulated a 'Just World' theory which suggests that people have an inherent belief that the world is an orderly, predictable and just place. However, when disaster strikes and what appear to be innocent people suffer, this causes cognitive dissonance and confusion in the witness. To resolve this, and preserve his or her belief in a just world, the witness apportions blame to the victim and perceives him or her as bringing the disaster on him or herself. This is believed to be responsible for the apparent lack of sympathy sometimes evidenced in the law courts and press for those who are really innocent victims of crime.

If this were also the case when, for example, the healing miracles took place, it could even have been accepted by the afflicted

4. *Miracles and Miracle Stories*, 549–60.

5. *Miracles and the New Testament*, 43–59.

6. *Signs, Miracles and Wonders*, 19–37.

7. *Just World Research and the Attribution Process*, 1030–51.

themselves that they had somehow sinned and deserved to be in that condition. Thus, the voice of authority forgiving that person of their sins could have been an important step in the healing process. Trench (1850)[8] provides some confirmation of this by pointing out that in biblical times both leprosy and blindness were seen as a punishment for sin. Therefore, for this and the other reasons mentioned, many witnesses of Jesus' miracles may have had presuppositions and expectations that encouraged them to accept events as supernatural which otherwise they may have regarded as rational and unremarkable. If this is indeed the case, even with some of the miracle reports, then the Gospel accounts may not always be unbiased and neutral.

With regard to the four Gospels that contain accounts of the miracles with which this enquiry is concerned, that of Matthew is generally attributed to the disciple of the same name, who would thus have had first-hand knowledge of Jesus and his activities. It is suggested that the Gospel was penned before 62 AD, but some think later. Woods (2007)[9] opines that the Jewish content of Matthew argues for its priority, since the early church was primarily Jewish and the text suggests that the writer had a Jewish audience in mind. He emphasizes Jesus' role as a teacher (e.g. "go and learn what this means" Matt 9:13) and seeks to appeal to the readers that the OT prophesies had been fulfilled in Jesus, that he was the new Messiah and, through him, the Kingdom of God had 'broken into' this world (Van den Brink, 1997)[10]. However, In reviewing the 'Synoptic problem' (a term used to describe the study of, and attempted explanation of, the similarities and differences between the first three Gospels), McKnight (1988)[11] favors the 'Oxford hypothesis' that Matthew and Luke both drew on Mark's account (regarded by many as the earliest), and an earlier postulated document usually designated 'Q'.

8. *The Cleansing of the Leper*, 209–21

9. *The Purpose of Matthew's Gospel*, 5–19.

10. *www.elim.nl/theologymatthew.html*

11. *The Synoptic Problem*, 36.

Butler (2001)[12] states that tradition favors Luke as the author of the gospel bearing his name, and also of Acts. He adds that Luke was a Gentile physician, citing "Our dear friend Luke, the doctor" (Col 4:14, NIV). Additionally, Morris (1999)[13] points to examples of medical language, including "*high* fever" (Luke, 4:38), and "*full* of leprosy" (5:12, NKJV). Luke's writings were probably written in the early 60s AD, especially as no event later than 62 AD is mentioned (Butler, 2001[14]; Morris, 1999[15]). Luke was not an eye-witness of Jesus, but his declared intention was to compile an orderly account, drawing on all the evidence he could find (1:1–4, NIV). His audience was probably Gentile enquirers and Christians who needed strengthening in their faith.

The author of Mark is anonymous, but he is commonly believed to be (John) Mark, son of Mary, in whose home in Jerusalem the believers met (Acts 12:12) (Moule, 1978)[16]. He was too young to have been an eye-witness (Cole, 2011)[17] but travelled with both Paul and Barnabas (the latter being one of his relatives, Col 4:10). He was with Peter in Rome during the later years ("My son Mark", 1 Pet 5:13) and may have even penned the latter's account of Jesus. Mark's gospel could have been written around the time of Peter's death in about 64 AD and, as noted above, some believe it was the first Gospel to be written. Guthrie (1970)[18] considers that Mark wrote for Gentiles in Rome to proclaim the Good News of Jesus and to encourage those who faced persecution, whilst Cole (2011)[19] adds that he was endeavoring to show the Roman authorities that Christians posed no threat.

The fourth Gospel, that of John, was probably the last to be written, being completed in its present form in the late eighties

12. *Luke*, 402–3.
13. *Authorship*, 16–24.
14. *Luke*, 402–3.
15. Ibid
16. *The Author*, 4–5.
17. *Author*, 946–47.
18. *Purpose and Readers*, 57–63.
19. *Purpose of the Gospel*, 947–48.

or early nineties AD. It is held to have been authored, along with some other New Testament books, by the apostle John, who would thus have been an eye-witness. In fact Guthrie (1970)[20] opines that John's statement "We have seen his glory" (1:14) implies that he was among the witnesses to Jesus' works. The book contains only occasional overlaps with the Synoptic Gospels, and differs from them in several respects: for instance it does not mention the birth of Jesus or the twelve disciples (Butler, 2011)[21]. The entire second half of the Gospel deals with just the last few days of Jesus' life and resurrection. The miracles are referred to as 'signs'; only eight are described, with six being unique to this Gospel. As Guthrie (2011)[22] observes, John himself makes the purpose of his Gospel clear in 20:31 "But these are written that you may believe that Jesus is the Messiah . . ." In other words, it was intended as an evangelistic instrument to produce faith in Jesus as Christ and Son of God. No intended audience is mentioned, but the book may have been written for his colleagues in Asia Minor where he worked after Jesus' death, or simply for a general readership.

Jesus performed more miracles than are individually described in these Gospels, as suggested by: "[Jesus] healed all who were ill" (Matt 8:16), "all who touched it [the edge of His cloak] were healed" (Matt 14:36), and "Jesus did many other things as well." (John 21:25). Additionally, there are passing allusions to other works: "some women who had been cured of evil spirits and diseases" (Luke 8:2), and "I will keep driving out demons and healing people today and tomorrow" (Luke 14:32).

Whilst there seems to be consensus among commentators regarding thirty-one specific miracles reported in the four Gospels, there are differing views on the complete list, ranging up to a total of forty-five. Some commentators include one or more of the aforementioned generalizations, or events that applied to Jesus himself, such as his virgin birth, transfiguration and resurrection, as well as Jesus passing unseen through the crowd (Luke 4:30). In

20. *Self-indications in the Gospel*, 242–44.

21. *John, Gospel of*, 362–64.

22. *Purpose*, 1022.

addition to these, Wright (1927)[23] also included Jesus' cleansing of the temple (Matt 21:12), and the falling of soldiers (John 18:6). Blackburn (2011)[24] added the reference in Luke 8:2 to Mary Magdalene having been previously exorcised, but no details of the actual event are provided by the evangelist. The story of the demons of the man at Gerasenes entering pigs, followed by the pigs drowning themselves in the lake (Mark 5:11–13), is sometimes listed as two separate miracles. Conversely, Trench (1850)[25] omits both the healing of the man unable to speak (Matt 9:33) and the blind and mute man (Matt 12:22), whilst Wright (1927)[26] omits the healing of a possessed boy (Matt 17:18) and the post-resurrection miraculous catch of fish (John 21:6).

The present study will exclude the events that happened to Jesus himself, the generalizations, and those added by Wright (1927)[27] and Blackburn (2011)[28], but will include the four omitted by Trench (1850)[29] and Wright (1927)[30]. The final total of thirty-five includes the thirty-one on which there is already consensus, and provides a list of specific miracles that are described in sufficient detail to enable at least some level of investigation to take place.

---

23. *Miracles*, 186–91.

24. *The Miracles of Jesus*, 119.

25. *Miracles*, 95–475.

26. *Miracles*, 186–91.

27. Ibid.

28. *The Miracles of Jesus*, 119.

29. *Miracles*, 95–475.

30. *Miracles*, 186–91.

CHAPTER 4

CATEGORIES OF MIRACLES,
AND PROCEDURE

SEVERAL COMMENTATORS HAVE DIVIDED the miracles into categories to aid subsequent discussion. For example Wright (1927)[1] firstly delineates: (1) miracles of nature (the changing of water into wine, Jesus walking on water, etc), (2) miracles of man (the healings), and (3) miracles of the spirit world (exorcisms). He also suggests an alternative classification into eight categories, where the healings are divided into four clusters, the nature miracles into three, and with the raising of the dead as the final division. Blackburn's (1992)[2] discussion is restricted to just two categories: healings/exorcisms, and nature miracles/raising the dead. Within the latter, however, he separately considers "provision miracles" (changing water into wine, and feeding the multitudes), and "rescue miracles" (Jesus' calming of, and walking on, the water).

For the present study, the thirty-five miracles that will be investigated can be broadly categorized as follows:

Healings = 17
Exorcisms = 6
Raising of the dead = 3
Controlling nature = 9

1. *Miracles*, 186–91.
2. *Miracles and Miracle Stories*, 549–60.

Table 1 shows the complete list of miracles and categories, with Gospel references.

Table 1
Thirty-five Gospel miracles, categories, first reference, and parallels

No.	Category/Miracle	Gospel Ref.	Parallels
-	**Healings**	-	-
1	Official's son	John 4:46–54	None
2	Peter's mother-in-law	Matt 8:14–15	Mark & Luke
3	Man with leprosy	Matt 8:1–4	Mark & Luke
4	Centurion's servant	Matt 8:5–13	Luke
5	A paralytic	Matt 9:1–7	Mark & Luke
6	Withered hand	Matt 12:9–14	Mark & Luke
7	Woman with bleeding	Matt 9:20–22	Mark & Luke
8	Two blind men	Matt 9:27–31	None
9	Invalid at Bethesda	John 5:1–15	None
10	Deaf and dumb man	Mark 7:31–37	None
11	Blind man at Bethsaida	Mark 8:22–26	None
12	Man born blind	John 9:1–12	None
13	Crippled woman	Luke 13:10–17	None
14	Man with dropsy	Luke 14:1–6	None
15	Ten lepers	Luke 17:11–19	None
16	Blind Bartimaeus	Matt 20:29–34	Mark & Luke
17	Servant's severed ear	Luke 22:50–51	None

No.	Category/Miracle	Gospel Ref.	Parallels
-	**Exorcisms**	-	-
1	Man at Capernaum	Mark 1:21–27	Luke
2	Demons transferred to pigs	Matt 8:28–33	Mark & Luke
3	Man unable to speak	Matt 9:32–34	None
4	Demon-possessed daughter	Matt 15:21–28	Mark
5	Boy with a demon	Matt 17:14–20	Mark & Luke
6	Blind, mute demonic	Matt 12:22–23	Mark & Luke
-	**Raising of the Dead**	-	-
1	Widow's son in Nain	Luke 7:11–17	None
2	Jairus' daughter	Matt 9:18, 23–26	Mark & Luke
3	Lazarus	John 11:1–45	None
-	**Controlling Nature**	-	-
1	Changing water into wine	John 2:1–11	None
2	First catch of fish	Luke 5:1–11	None
3	Calming the storm	Matt 8:23–27	Mark & Luke
4	Feeding the 5,000	Matt 14:13–21	Mark, Luke, John
5	Jesus walks on water	Matt 14:22–33	Mark & John
6	Feeding the 4,000	Matt 15:32–39	Mark
7	Coin in fish's mouth	Matt 17:24–27	None
8	Withering of the fig tree	Matt 21:18–22	Mark
9	Second catch of fish	John 21:4–11	None

The nature of the illnesses cured is not always made explicit. The highest category of those identified is blindness (four), and two are of leprosy. Paralysis is mentioned in two cases, and fever also in two. The other conditions are cited just once in each case, and one remains unspecified. Some healings were of several people at once, but these are treated as single incidents for the purpose of this study. Table 2 shows these details in full.

Table 2
Illnesses that were cured

No.	Illness	First Gospel ref.
-	**Blindness**	-
1	Two blind men	Matt 9:27–31
2	Blind man at Bethsaida	Mark 8:22–26
3	Man born blind	John 9:1–12
4	Blind Bartimaeus	Matt 20:29–34
-	**Leprosy**	-
1	Man with leprosy	Matt 8:1–4
2	Ten lepers	Luke 17:11–19
-	**Paralysis**	-
1	Centurion's servant	Matt 8:5–13
2	Paralyzed man on a mat	Matt 9:1–7
-	**Fever**	-
1	Official's son about to die (fever?)	John 4:46–54
2	Peter's mother-in law	Matt 8:14–15
-	**Bleeding**	-
1	Woman with bleeding (gynecological?)	Matt 9:20–22
-	**Withered Hand**	-
1	Man with this condition	Matt 12:9–14
-	**Deaf and Dumb**	-
1	Deaf and dumb man	Matt 7:31–37
-	**Crippled**	-
1	Crippled woman	Luke 13:10–17
-	**Dropsy**	-
1	Man with dropsy	Luke 14:1–6

No.	Illness	First Gospel ref.
-	**Severed Ear**	-
1	Servant's severed ear	Luke 22:50–51
-	**Unspecified**	-
1	Invalid at Bethesda	John 5:1–15

Identifying the purpose behind miracles and the reasons they were performed may inform subsequent attempts to explain their workings. Brown (2011)[3] points out that Jesus had been accused of being a false prophet and of using signs and wonders in order to lead people astray, which was a capital offence in those days. This warning was expressed in Deut 13:2–3: "if the sign or wonder takes place, and the prophet says 'Let us follow other gods' . . . you must not listen to (him) . . . (he) must be put to death". That this nearly happened is described in John 10:25–39, with the report that the Jews were ready to stone Jesus saying (v. 33): "We are not stoning you for any good work . . . but for blasphemy, because you, a mere man, claim to be God." Jesus tries to assure them that he is doing the works of his father, God, but they are not convinced. He does, however, manage to escape on that occasion.

Thus, these Jews misunderstood Jesus' miracles and were not convinced of his authenticity or that his powers came from the True God. Other healers and magicians were operating at that time, but their 'miracles' did not serve a higher purpose, as did those of Jesus (Trench, 1850)[4]. As noted by Olander (2006)[5], there was always a specific grounding to Jesus' miracles, and cites in support of this the statement in John 3:2 that no one could perform the signs Jesus was doing if God were not with him, This is supported in Acts 2:22 when Peter says: "Jesus of Nazareth was a man

---

3. *Issues in the History and Debates on Miracles*, 273.

4. *Assults on the Miracles: The Heathen*, 60–63.

5. *Signs, Miracles and Wonders*, 19–37.

accredited by God to you by miracles, wonders and signs, which God did . . . through him."

In a more comprehensive consideration of the purpose of Jesus' miracles, Wright (1927)[6] lists five pertinent characteristics. Firstly, they were spontaneous, mostly unplanned and arose from the occasion; secondly they had a high moral purpose and were never an end in themselves; thirdly they were not used for personal gain; fourthly they were in keeping with the moral dignity and innermost nature of Jesus and; fifthly, they were designed to relieve suffering and reveal his divine love and pity.

In similar vein Erickson (1985)[7] suggests three purposes for the miracles: to glorify God (which is what the beneficiaries generally did after witnessing one); to establish the supernatural basis for the revelation that often accompanied these 'signs' and, as in Wright's offering, to show compassion and meet human needs. In summary, therefore, the evidence points to Jesus performing his miracles not for personal gain or aggrandizement, but to proclaim the coming of the Kingdom of God and the related presentation of himself as a teacher (Blackburn, 2011)[8], and out of genuine compassion to help people in need as the occasions demanded.

The procedure used for investigating the miracles is as follows. The seventeen specific healing miracles reported in the Gospels are examined first, followed by the six exorcisms, the three raisings from the dead and, lastly, the nine "nature" miracles. The process follows the four stages described below, and is based mostly on the writer's personal interpretations and knowledge as a Chartered Psychologist. In addition, the analyses will include the views of Dr David Major on the medical symptoms described in the accounts of some of the healing miracles. Dr Major is a physician and also a qualified Reader in the Church of England. These contributions are acknowledged in the text where applicable. The opinions of other scholars are largely ignored during examination

6. *Miracles*, 186–91.

7. *Providence and Miracles*, 409.

8. *Jesus' Understanding of his Miracles*, 120–4.

of the healing, exorcism and raising miracles, but are taken into account in the final section dealing with the "nature" miracles.

(1) Is the report accurate and reliable?

The New International Bible (NIV) (2011) is the default biblical text used for the initial reading of the miracle accounts, as this incorporates the latest findings from many manuscript fragments and is considered ideal for study purposes. These readings are then compared with two other interpretations: the more liberal Good News Bible (GNB) and also the more traditional New King James Version (NKJV), as they are sometimes based on different ancient codices and can thus provide additional details or clarification. Finally, *The New Greek – English Interlinear New Testament* (1990, edited by J. D. Douglas) is consulted and the meanings of key Greek words cross-checked in the *Lexicon* (Friberg et al., 2005).

The aim of these steps is to obtain the most accurate under-standing possible of what actually occurred. Factors affecting the reliability and accuracy of the reporting were discussed earlier and, in the analyses that follow, the confidence in an account will be strengthened: if there are parallel versions in more than one Gospel, if there were many witnesses to the reported miracle, especially if these include one or more Gospel writers, and by there being several similar examples. This will help to form an opinion on whether or not the particular reports would be acceptable as evidence, according to the legalistic definition discussed by Anonymous (1914)[9].

(2) Is there a naturalistic explanation?

A miracle for which there appears to be accurate and reliable evidence will be examined to see if there could be a rational explanation. If it can be seen as a naturalistic event that occurred at an opportune time, this would not rule out a supernatural intervention to bring this about where and when it happened.

9. *"Studies in Theology" and Hume's "Essays on Miracles"*, 105–31.

Whether or not this is believed to be the case would be a matter of faith rather than logic.

(3) Was evidence missed?

Where an event has no naturalistic explanation, the possibility that the reporter missed additional evidence that could have provided a simple or rational explanation will be explored. If this is possible or probable, then the decision regarding divine intervention still remains a matter of faith as per stage two.

(4) Is the explanation supernatural, or allegorical/symbolic?

If none of the previous steps yields a likely explanation, we are left with the possibilities that the event was either a true miracle of God—one that could not have occurred without a supernatural manipulation of nature—or it was allegorical or symbolic and not meant to be taken literally. This process is summarized in Figure 1.

Figure 1
Flowchart of Miracle Analysis Scheme

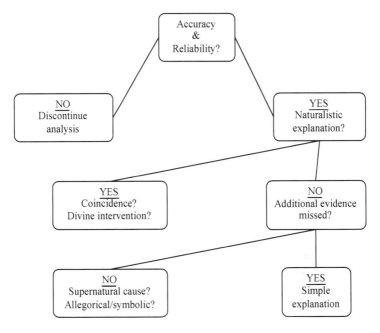

It should be emphasized that the final verdicts are purely those of the present writer. The reader is free to formulate his or her own explanations according to the facts presented. These could include the view that all the biblical accounts are inerrant and that all the miracles should be accepted as being enacted by God through Jesus exactly as described.

As mentioned in chapter 1, this analytical process follows the principles of the "supported philosophical-deductive approach". Rather than trying to support a premise, which in the present case would be that miracles are supernaturalistic events, evidence is sought to support a series of alternate premises to discount this. If an alternate premise is not supported then the original one stands, not because it has been "proved" but because it has survived attempts to "disprove" it. The examination of each miracle will conclude with a verdict summarizing what the evidence suggests is the most likely explanation.

CHAPTER 5

CONSIDERATIONS CONCERNING HEALING MIRACLES

BEFORE CONSIDERING THE HEALING of specific medical conditions, it is necessary to differentiate between those that result from physical damage or abnormality, such as a broken limb or a cancerous organ, from those that may have a psychological cause. This is because it is more credible to accept naturalistic cures for the latter rather than for the former, and thus it has an impact on many of the healing cases to be examined. The list of bodily ailments that can have psychosomatic causes is extensive, and includes asthma, heart disease, diabetes, skin diseases and tuberculosis (Kaplan & Sadock, 1981)[1]. In addition, there are 'conversion disorders', which Kaplan and Sadock define as "a group of disorders in which the essential features are physical symptoms suggesting physical illness . . . for which there are no demonstrable organic findings to explain the symptoms."

According to Sigmund Freud's original theory, what he called "hysterical neurosis" is triggered by emotionally traumatic events that are consciously repressed as a way of managing the pain, and the resulting emotional charge is "converted" into neurological symptoms. This then helps to relieve the mental symptoms, but it may also gratify dependency needs. A surprising range of physical

1. *Modern Synopsis of Comprehensive Textbook of Psychiatry/iii*, 453

conditions can result from such conversion disorders, including paralysis, abnormal and convulsive movements such as tremors, fainting, impairment or loss of speech, and sensory symptoms including impaired vision, hearing, and touch. Where a condition has a psychological origin, then a "faith" cure that is accomplished without medication or surgery remains a possibility.

There is also the phenomenon known as psychoneuroimmunology (PNI)—the link between psychological processes such as the emotions, brain function, and the immune response that plays a significant role in physical illness. The term was first used by Ader and Cohen (1975)[2], but the origins of the modern understanding of PNI can be traced back to earlier observations of physical changes that accompany emotional states. As an example of negative consequences, Seyle (1956)[3] described a process he called the 'General Adaptation Syndrome' where, in response to physical or psychological stress, the hypothalamus mediates the secretion of adrenocorticotropic hormone (ACTH) by the pituitary, which in turn results in the adrenal gland releasing adrenal corticoids. Whilst this may be helpful in the short term, if the problem persists, the resulting heightened alert condition may be prolonged and lead to impairment of the body's immune system. This in turn can cause a range of serious physical conditions including atrophy of various organs, gastric ulcerations, proneness to infections, slow wound healing, and ultimately even death.

By contrast, a positive example of PNI at work is that, if we are happy we may laugh, and laughing has a number of health benefits. Keith-Spiegel (1972)[4] summarized the views of earlier writers in stating that laughter ". . . restores homeostasis, stabilizes blood pressure, oxygenates the blood, massages the vital organs, stimulates circulation, [and] facilitates digestion . . . ." In addition to these physical benefits, laughing facilitates the release of a number of health-giving hormones. These include: catecholamines, which improve alertness, stimulate memory, and reduce

2. *Behaviorally Conditioned Immunosuppression*, 333–40.

3. *The Stress of Life*

4. *Early Conceptions of Humor: Varieties and Issues*, 3–35.

inflammation; endorphins, the body's natural opiates that enhance positive mood, control pain, and stimulate the immune system; and immunoglobulin "A" which protects against upper respiratory tract infections. Also, the activity of white blood cells and T-cells are increased, thus enhancing the ability to fight infections (Lally, 1991[5]; Holden, 1993[6]).

A famous example of PNI at work some years ago concerned Norman Cousins (1979[7]) who claimed relief, and even cure, from what was believed to be ankylosing spondylitis, by watching comedy films from his hospital bed. An anecdotal story related to this concerns Cousins asking Nobel laureate Albert Schweitzer, who had built a hospital in Gabon, Africa, if he objected to people visiting witch doctors when professional medical help was already available. Schweitzer is reported to have replied that he had no problem with that, as we each have a doctor within us and a good healer just opens the way for this doctor within to do its own good work.

Another aspect that may influence healing is the effect that a strong faith in God can have on one's physical and mental health. Significant research on this was carried out by Koenig (2001[8]; 2002[9]). He found that religious beliefs may provide people with a form of control over health matters that their non-religious peers do not have, because religious people pray to God believing that he is capable of intervening—thus they can *do* something to help improve their situation. Amazingly, his surveys found that religious activities might even be associated with an enhanced longevity of up to seven years. However, a later study by Ardelt and Koenig (2006)[10] showed that the main benefits lay with people who had "intrinsic religious orientation" (where religion is a major

5. *Laugh your Stress Away*, 50–52.

6. *Laughter is the Best Medicine*, 40–42.

7. *Anatomy of an Illness—as Perceived by the Patient*

8. *The healing Power of Faith*

9. *A Commentary: The Role of Religion and Spirituality at the End of Life*, 20–23

10. *The Role of Religion for Hospice Patients and Relatively Healthy Older Adults*, 184–205.

motivation for how one lives and understands one's life) rather than those with "extrinsic religious orientation" (where religion is used for one's own ends). The notion that religious faith may play a part in reports of miraculous healings is supported by other scholars, including Keener (2011)[11] who notes that the power of faith can result in a reduction in anxiety and an increase in well-being, and Hvidt (2011)[12] who states that faith in miracles can often be helpful as a coping resource.

One final factor concerning the healing miracles is that the biblical reports are generally limited to "here and now" events, with minimal background such as the duration or cause of an illness or the evidence of a permanent cure. Whilst it would have clearly been impractical for the Gospel writers to provide long-term follow-up to the healings, it does result in the possibility that some cures were not permanent.

11. *Factors in Healthy Religious Practice*, 625–30.
12. *Patient Belief in Miraculous Healing*, 309–29.

CHAPTER 6

HEALING: BLINDNESS

First Case

THERE ARE FOUR EXAMPLES reported in the Gospels, with the first appearing only in Matthew (9:27–31). Two blind men asked Jesus to cure them; he asked them if they believed that he could accomplish this, and they said "Yes". Jesus touched their eyes and said it would be done according to their faith, and their sight was restored. The NKJV has the same key words as the NIV, and the GNB differs only in Jesus saying that it would be done as they "believed" (cf. their "faith"). The narrative is straight forward, and there are no ambiguities with the Greek translation: *tuphloi* means blind, without sight, *pisteuete* means believe, be convinced, and *ēpsato* means touch, take hold.

This miracle does not fully satisfy the reliability criterion due to a lack of parallel versions and the absence of witnesses, although it is likely that some of the disciples travelling with Jesus were present. There are, however, several other examples of restoring sight that lend some support to this Gospel account, so further examination of the present case might inform the others. The text does not reveal details of the cause of the blindness or its duration, although it does state that the two men were "following" Jesus; could this mean that at least one of them might have been partly sighted, or that somebody was guiding them, in order to keep pace with Jesus?

There are many causes of blindness, including physical conditions such as cataract, trachoma, diabetic retinopathy, and macular degeneration. For Jesus to cure conditions like these instantly by nothing more than a touch would indicate supernatural powers. As mentioned in the previous section, however, impaired vision can also result from a psychological "conversion disorder", a condition that used to be known as "hysterical blindness" and, in principle, it could have responded to a psychological cure. If this were the case with the two men, then the healing might have been accomplished by naturalistic means. The individuals confirmed that they had faith that Jesus could heal them, so they were mentally prepared for this to be done, and Jesus reinforced the "faith" healing by performing the physical action of touching their eyes, a sign that something had been done.

Verdict: According to the principles of this investigation, and in the absence of more specific details of the disability, an alternative premise—that this cure of blindness could have been made through naturalistic means, albeit engineered by Jesus and helped by the faith the men had— negates the certainty of a supernaturalistic intervention.

Second Case

Again this is only reported in one Gospel, this time in Mark (8:22–26). A blind man was brought to Jesus whilst he and his disciples were at Bethsaida. Jesus took the man outside the village and used both spittle and touch on his eyes to restore his sight. This was done in two stages and, after the first, Jesus asked the man if he could see anything. The man replied "I see people; they look like trees walking around" (8:24). After Jesus repeated the procedure, the man's sight was fully restored. The accounts in the GNB and NKJV concur, and again the Greek key words are unambiguous: *ptusas* means spit, *epethēken cheiras* means lay on hands.

As with the first example, the reliability is limited by the single Gospel account and the dearth of witnesses, but the inclusion of the detail of the man initially seeing people "like trees walking" adds to the authenticity: it is a credible reaction to partial sight restoration. Although the note that Jesus led the man away suggests total blindness, again no cause, or duration of, the condition is provided. In view of the fact that the man recognized trees and people indicates that his visual cortex was developed and thus he had not been born blind. His affliction might therefore have been relatively recent, with either a physical cause such as trachoma, as suggested by Dr Major, or some severe conjunctivitis, or even a psychosomatic origin. This time there is no mention of Jesus enquiring about the man's faith but, in addition to the physical touching of the eyes, spittle was applied that could have had some cleansing effect.

Verdict: As with the first case, the blindness could have been cured by naturalistic rather than supernaturalistic means.

Third Case

Again there is only one report, this time in John 9:1–12. However, the details are more specific in that they state that the man was born blind, but do not mention whether or not he asked to be cured or was asked if he had faith. Spittle was again used, but this time it was mixed with mud and applied to the man's eyes. The man was told to wash in the Pool of Siloam, and after doing this he could see. The GNB account is similar, but emphasizes that the mud poultice was *rubbed* on the man's eyes, whereas the NKJB refers to it as *anointing* the eyes. The Greek *epechrisen* can be translated as either smear on, anoint, or rub in, and *pēlon* as clay or mud.

Although the disciples may have been the only witnesses to the healing, many people, including the man's parents, saw that the man who had been a beggar was now cured. Whilst this is only a single Gospel account, the many witnesses after the event lends some reliability to the story, especially as they appear to confirm that the man had been blind from birth. Other details, however, remain unknown. If the man really had been congenitally blind then, as mentioned above concerning the second case, his visual cortex would not have developed and so just healing his eyes would not have restored sight.

Verdict: Either this was a case of supernatural intervention affecting the brain as well as the eyes, or there is an allegorical explanation in that the man was spiritually blind but now his "eyes had been opened" by Jesus.

Fourth Case

This is recorded in all three Synoptic Gospels. Matthew's version (20:29–34) bears some similarity to the first example in that two blind men called out to Jesus as he was passing and, despite resistance from the crowd, asked to be able to see. Jesus touched their eyes, and they were healed. In this instance, there was a "large crowd" present as witnesses, as well as the disciples. The other two Gospel accounts differ from Matthew's in that Mark (10:46–52) and Luke (18:35–43) both refer to just one blind man, whom Mark alone names Bartimaeus. They do not mention that Jesus touched the man's eyes, but do add that he said "your faith has made you well" (Mark) or "has saved you" (Luke). The accounts differ on whether Jesus was leaving, was at, or was approaching Jericho, but all state that he healed man or men then followed Jesus.

The GNB versions are substantially the same, but Luke this time concurs with Mark in stating "has made you well", as does the NKJV. The Greek *pistis* means confidence, faith, or trust, *aneblepsen* means to have recovered his sight. The reliability of this example gains from the many witnesses and the parallel accounts, but differences especially between Matthew's account and those of the other two, shed some doubt on its accuracy. The main ambiguities concern whether the party was arriving at or leaving Jericho, whether there was one blind man or two, and whether Jesus touched the eyes or just spoke to the afflicted. Matthew was the only one of the three authors who could have witnessed the event, but his memory might have faded between then and the time of writing; the other two writers could have drawn from a different source (the postulated 'Q' document?). Only Mark names the man as Bartimaeus. Again we are not given details of the causes of the blindness or its duration.

Verdict: This healing may have been by naturalistic means, especially as Jesus commented that faith had made the man or men well. There is also a possible allegory in that the man or men were being rewarded for overcoming resistance from the crowd in reaching Jesus.

CHAPTER 7

HEALING: LEPROSY AND PARALYSIS

Leprosy (two examples)

First Case

THIS IS REPORTED IN all three Synoptic Gospels. Matthew (8:1–4) states that large crowds were following Jesus, and a man with leprosy approached him and said that, if he chose to do so, he could make him clean. Jesus touched the man, and he was cleansed. Mark's (1:40–45) account is essentially the same but the crowds are not mentioned. Luke (5:12–14) adds the man was "covered" with leprosy, and that the event took place in a town. All three accounts in the GNB refer to a "dreaded skin disease" rather than specifically leprosy, whilst the NKJV retains the specific name. The Greek *lepra*, whilst it can mean leprosy, was probably also used for a variety of skin diseases. Similarly *lepros* originally meant scaly or scabby as well as leprous.

In Matthew's version the crowds who were following Jesus would presumably have been witnesses to this healing, as might people who were in the town cited by Luke. Apart from this, again only some disciples were likely to have been present. We have no details of the duration of the man's ailment, but only the comment by Luke that it was extensive. Whilst leprosy is the term generally used for the medical condition involved in this miracle, as the Greek word indicates, it does not necessarily always imply this specific disease, and the GNB version reflects this. Leprosy itself is a bacterial infection caused by *Mycobacterium leprae*, which requires extensive prolonged treatment with a cocktail of modern antibiotics. Other skin conditions include syphilis and psoriasis, as suggested by Dr Major, and the severity of the latter can be influenced by one's state of emotional well-being.

The sufferer had faith that Jesus could cure him and, as he had done on other occasions, Jesus touched the man to signify a healing act. Thus a naturalistic "faith" cure is at least a possibility, although this would be influenced by the specific nature of the disease. However, whilst restoration of sight by any means could in principle be instant, it would be remarkable if extensive skin lesions disappeared "immediately" —the term used by each of the three evangelists reporting this event—regardless of their cause. Leprosy, like its related disease tuberculosis, could go into remission with care and healthy living but this is a long-term solution. Only Matthew could have witnessed the healing first hand, and some fading memory along with subsequent redaction of the story may have occurred.

Verdict: If the accounts of an instant cure are accurate, especially if the disease was genuine leprosy, then this would indicate a supernaturalistic event.

Second Case

This concerns the healing of ten lepers, and is only reported by Luke (17:11–19), which reduces the reliability and accuracy of the case. The men asked for pity, and Jesus only spoke to them "at a distance", telling them to go and show themselves to the priests. As they went, we are told that they were cleansed, although only one man returned to Jesus to say so. It may be relevant that Jesus called the one who had returned "a foreigner". There was no physical contact, but the sufferers apparently had faith that they could be cured. The GNB and NKJV accounts are similar, and the Greek term used for leprosy is the same as that used previously, and could have included a range of skin ailments. Luke's account would have been from second-hand sources, and the details are minimal with no other witnesses being mentioned apart from, presumably, some of the disciples.

A person with leprosy was considered "unclean" and could not enter synagogues. If he or she believed they had been cured, they would have had to show themselves to the priest to confirm this, as required by Levitical tradition (see Lev 14:2), and this is what Jesus commanded. The narrative only confirms that one man returned to confirm he was cured, and he obviously recognized Jesus—the son of God—as the source of his healing. If the others had also been cured, then they may have attached greater importance to salvation through works (of the law) than through faith in the Lord.

Verdict: Both natural and supernatural explanations are possible for this healing, although the reliability of the facts is not strong. There may be a suggestion of allegory here, in that many people do not recognize the source of the good things that happen to them. It is also possible that, in referring to the one who returned as a "a foreigner" the Gospel writer was suggesting that the Jews had not accepted Jesus as the Messiah, and were preoccupied with the law, whereas at least some Gentiles (as exemplified by the one who returned) had become converts. Paul, in the book of Romans and elsewhere, makes many references to Gentile converts and Jewish reticence.

Paralysis (two examples)

First Case

There are two accounts of this miracle. According to Matthew (8:5–13), a centurion approached Jesus saying that his servant at home was paralyzed. Jesus said he would come and cure him but the centurion said it was not necessary; that it only needed Jesus to "speak the word". Jesus did so, and the servant was cured at that time. Luke's account (7:1–10) differs in some detail: the sufferer is described as a slave, and the illness is not specified but was serious, and the man was close to death; the centurion did not personally speak to Jesus, but sent others to do so on his behalf. Whilst the NKJV agrees with the versions in the NIV, the GNB translation of Matthew has a Roman officer refer to a servant who is sick in bed unable to move, but otherwise concurs with the account in Luke. The Greek *ekatontarchos*, meaning a centurion is used in both Gospels, but the patient is described as his *pais*, meaning a child, in Matthew but *doulos*, his slave in Luke. The patient's condition is described as *paralutikos*, meaning paralyzed in the former, and *kakōs*, meaning badly ill or sick in the latter.

This healing is unusual in that there was no contact between Jesus and the patient. Although the two accounts use different terms for the patient (*pais* and *doulos*), in a culture where the master of the house was all-powerful, they could be regarded as interchangeable. However, the lack of close agreement between the two Gospel versions on the type of illness, and the lack of witnesses, must cast some doubt on the accuracy and reliability of this miracle account. The fact that the centurion was so concerned might indicate a sudden onset of the illness. Dr Major suggests that a possible diagnosis could be neuritis that leads to paralysis, from which rapid improvement is sometimes possible. It could also conceivably have been a conversion disorder from which a spontaneous or naturalistic cure can occur. This does not, however, rule out a medical condition that required supernatural intervention for rapid cure. The story might also be an allegory for those who have faith without needing the physical presence of Jesus, as he does take the opportunity of inserting a short homily (Matt 8:10–12) stating that those in Israel with little faith will be cast outside the Kingdom of Heaven and replaced by people from the "East and the West".

Verdict: This is most likely a naturalistic cure, or an allegory, but a supernatural intervention is still possible, especially as this was a 'remote' healing.

Second Case

This is paralleled in each of the Synoptic Gospels. Matthew (9:1–7) states that people brought to Jesus a paralyzed man lying on a bed. Jesus "saw" their faith and told the man that his sins were forgiven. He then told the man to stand up, take his bed, and go home, which he did. Mark (2:1–12) and Luke (5:17–26) both provide the additional details that the event took place in a house and that there were so many people present that the patient had to be lowered through the roof. Luke alone adds that the power of the Lord to heal was with Jesus. There are no significant differences with the GNB and NKJV versions. As in the first example, the same Greek word for paralyzed is used in all three accounts, and *piotis* is appropriately translated as faith, confidence, or trust.

This event gains in reliability and accuracy from the parallel accounts and the many witnesses. Again we do not know the cause or duration of the paralysis, but the same possible causes and cures may be suggested here as for the first example. The patient had faith that he would be cured and may have believed that his condition was caused by sinning, a not uncommon view in those times. When Jesus assured him that his sins were forgiven, and his authority to pronounce this was accepted, then a naturalistic "faith" cure might have been effected rather than a supernaturalistic one.

Verdict: This was most likely a naturalistic healing, aided by the man's faith and belief that his sins had been forgiven.

CHAPTER 8

HEALING: FEVER, BLEEDING AND WITHERED HAND

Fever (two examples)

First Case

ONLY JOHN (4:46–54) REPORTS this case. A royal official approached Jesus to say that his son was dying and would Jesus come and heal him. Jesus told the man to go and that his son would live. The father believed him, went home, and was told that the fever had left his son at the precise time of Jesus' pronouncement. The GNB version agrees, although refers to the man as a government official, whilst the NKJV calls him a nobleman. There are no anomalies with the key Greek words: *basilikos* means royal officer, *apothnēskein* means suffer death, and *puretos* means fever.

The reliability of this case suffers from a lack of parallel accounts, although John could himself have been an eyewitness. Apart from presumably other disciples, no other witnesses are mentioned. This is a further example of healing where, like the first paralysis example, Jesus did not have direct contact with the patient. No details of the illness are provided other than the mention of the "fever" disappearing. There could have been a range of causes, including microbial, viral or parasitic infection (including malaria with its raised temperature rigors), or visceral abscess. At least some features might have had a psychosomatic origin. An infection could have naturally run its course, but other conclusions are highly speculative due to a lack of additional detail. What is made explicit is that the father had faith, and the child became well before he had returned home.

Verdict: This could have been a natural recovery, but a supernatural intervention remains possible in view of the lack of direct contact.

Second Case

All three Synoptic Gospels report this. Mathew (8:14–15) states that Jesus entered Peter's house where his mother-in-law was lying in bed with a fever. He touched her hand and the fever left her, and she got up. Mark's version (1:29–31) is similar but adds that James and John were present, and that Jesus took the woman by the hand, lifted her up, and the fever departed. Luke (4:38–39) omits mention of James and John, although he uses the third person plural "they" implying that others were present. He adds that the woman had a *high* fever, and that Jesus stood over the woman and rebuked the fever which then left her.

The GNB version is similar except for substituting "ordered the fever to leave her" instead of "rebuked the fever" in Luke. The NKJV has "immediately the fever left her" instead of just "left her" in Mark's account, but in the Greek text *aphēken* means "left" without any implication of immediacy. Also in Mark, *ēgeiren* can mean "lifted up" but more literally means awakened or aroused, whilst Luke's mention of Jesus "rebuking" the fever is one meaning of *epetimēsen* along with appraise or charge.

The reliability of this account gains from the existence of parallel versions, although it is perhaps surprising that John does not also include this example as he is specifically named (in Mark) as a witness along with at least two or three other disciples. The three accounts between them provide reasonable detail, which adds to the accuracy. We are not given the reasons for the fever or its duration but, as with the first example, there could have been several causes including some of a psychological nature. Jesus performed actions to confirm that he was physically doing something, which probably included touching the patient, with or without lifting her, and challenging the fever.

Verdict: A naturalistic or "faith" cure is likely in this case, although a supernatural element can not be excluded.

Bleeding

For this and the remaining healing miracles there exists just a single example. This case of bleeding is reported in each of the Synoptic Gospels. Matthew's (9:20–22) account is short, stating that a woman who had been suffering from hemorrhages for twelve years touched the fringe of Jesus' cloak, believing that this would cure her. Jesus said that her faith had made her well, and she was healed. Mark 5:25–34 provides much additional detail, noting that the woman had consulted many physicians but could not be cured. Jesus felt power had gone out of him, and asked the crowd whom it was who had touched him. The woman nervously confessed and explained everything. Luke (8:43–48) also includes most of these details but adds that the woman confessed "in the presence of all the people."

The GNB prefers "bleeding" to "hemorrhaging" throughout, and Mark's version ends with the woman being cured of her "trouble". The NKJV refers to a "flow of blood" throughout and, in Mark's account, when the woman was healed it picturesquely states "the fountain of her blood was dried up" and ends with her being cured of her "affliction". The Greek key words are unambiguous: *haimorroousa* and *rusei haimatos* both translate as flow of blood or hemorrhage, *imatiou* as garment, *mastigos* as affliction or ailment, and both *esōthē* and *sōthsomai* as heal or cure.

The woman's affliction is usually taken to have been menorrhagia, which would have made her unclean in the eyes of the local populace, and thus she would have been reluctant to openly declare it. The story gains credibility due to the parallel accounts that between them provide much detail, and the many witnesses. Two points regarding the woman may, however, detract from the accuracy: she is reported to have "said to herself" that touching Jesus' cloak would heal her (Matthew) which is also implied by Luke, and the report that the hemorrhaging had stopped was, perhaps understandably, not confirmed by anyone but the woman herself. Nor is there confirmation of a permanent cure. Dr Major commented that, if the event coincided with the onset of menopause, then this would explain the cessation of blood flow, with or without the help of a faith cure. The woman clearly had a very strong faith.

Verdict: A supernaturalistic event cannot be excluded, but this time being enacted through the power residing within Jesus', but without his voluntary intervention. However, more medical details might indicate that the "cure" was a natural course of events.

Withered hand

The three Synoptic Gospels each report this. Matthew (12:9–14) states that Jesus and some disciples went into a synagogue and saw a man with a withered hand. Jesus told the man to stretch out his hand, and it was restored. A major point in this pericope is that those present believed it was unlawful to cure (i.e. work) on the Sabbath, but Jesus said that it was lawful to perform good deeds. Mark (3:1–6) adds that Jesus asked the man to come forward, whilst Luke (6:6–11) notes that it was the scribes and Pharisees who objected, that it was the right hand, and that it was "shriveled".

Whilst the NKJV version retains the key terms of the NIV, the GNB prefers "paralyzed" rather than "withered", and that the hand "became well" instead of was "restored". It also substitutes "teachers of the law" for "scribes" in Luke's version. The Greek *xēran* means paralyzed or useless as well as withered, *ekteinon* means stretch out, and *hapekatestathē* means restore.

The story gains in reliability and accuracy due to the combined parallel accounts and the many witnesses. There are several possible causes of this affliction, especially as the original Greek indicates that the hand could have been paralyzed or useless rather than withered in the literal sense. The diagnosis also depends on the duration, as a congenital or long-standing deformity such as cerebral palsy, as suggested by Dr Major, or 'claw hand' would be difficult if not impossible to cure by naturalistic or any other means, especially instantly. Alternatively, the condition could also have been due to a recent physical injury or temporary peripheral nerve damage or inflammation. If so, it is possible that forcing the hand to open ("stretch out"), even if painful, could have restored movement and shape.

There is, however, another pertinent point to this reported healing: that being the complaints from the scribes and Pharisees about healing on the Sabbath. It could be seen that Jesus goes out of his way to find someone to heal in the synagogue, right under their noses, in order to make his point about doing good work on the holy day when doing no work at all was the rule. There are further examples of such defiance in other healings (vide infra).

Verdict: In the absence of more detail, this could be supernaturalistic or naturalistic healing.

CHAPTER 9

VARIOUS OTHER HEALINGS

Deaf and dumb man

ONLY MARK (7:31–37) RELATES this example. People brought to Jesus a man who was deaf and could hardly talk and asked him to place his hands on him. Jesus took the man away from the crowd, put his fingers into his ears, then spat and touched his tongue. Jesus then looked up to heaven and said "be opened", and the man was able to speak plainly. The GNB and NKJV are substantially the same, although they refer to the speech problem as an impediment that was removed by the healing. In the Greek, *kōphon* means incapable of hearing, *mogilalon* means speaking with difficulty or stammering, and *eluthē* means set free or release.

Although Mark provides pertinent detail, the reliability is not helped by the healing being enacted away from the people, and there being only a single account of an event that Mark could not have personally witnessed. Although the man may have been completely deaf, he was not completely dumb and may merely have had a stammer. Details of the duration of the affliction are not provided but, as Dr Major notes, the deafness was probably not congenital as an undeveloped auditory cortex would have prevented restoration of hearing. Speech difficulties can arise from not being able to hear properly, and therefore not being able to copy words spoken by others, plus not having sensory feedback for one's own speech efforts. There are also possible psychosomatic causes for speech difficulties. It is not known whether Jesus removed any blockage from the man's ears when he inserted his fingers in them, or that the action was merely symbolic—as could have been the spitting and the touching of the man's tongue.

Verdict: Assuming this account is reliable, the evidence suggests a naturalistic cure.

Crippled woman

Luke (13:10–17) provides the only account of this miracle, and again it is one that takes place in a synagogue on the Sabbath. A woman was there who had been crippled "by a spirit" for eighteen years, was bent over and unable to straighten. Jesus put his hands on her and told her that she was set free from her infirmity, and she straightened up. Once again, as with the cure of the withered hand (vide supra) there was an adverse reaction from the leaders present. The GNB and NKJV versions agree with the NIV, except that the latter states the woman was "loosed" from her infirmity, rather than "set free". The Greek translations confirm the key words: *sugkuptousa* meaning disabled or bent over, *apolelusai* meaning set free or released, and *anōrthōthē* meaning to restore or straighten up.

Although this account is straight forward, reliability is limited by the minimal details and the single account. Dr Major notes that there are several causes of such severe stoops including scoliosis, ankylosing spondylitis, tuberculosis, osteoporosis, kyphosis ("dowager's hump"), and strain or injury. Most of these would be difficult to cure instantly by natural means, especially as the condition was chronic as implied by Luke's statement that the woman had suffered for eighteen years. Could there have been an accident or event that triggered the stooped condition?

Whilst it may have been possible to force the woman through the pain barrier to stand upright for the first time in years so that a trapped nerve or cramped muscles could be freed, a supernaturalistic cure can not be excluded. However, like the withered hand example, this healing was carried out on the Sabbath in defiance of the no work rule. Likewise the patient did not approach Jesus but was called forward by him, so it is just possible she might have been chosen because her condition was seen as amenable to instant cure.

Verdict: If this was an instant cure of a chronic condition, a supernaturalistic explanation is credible, but a "chosen" case amenable to a naturalistic cure cannot be ruled out.

Man with dropsy

Again this is only reported by Luke (14:1–6), who states that Jesus was eating at the house of a prominent Pharisee on the Sabbath, where he saw a man with an abnormal swelling of his body. Jesus asked the Pharisee if it was lawful to heal on the Sabbath, but received no reply. Notwithstanding this, Jesus took hold of the man and healed him. He then reiterated that people could do good deeds on the day of rest. The GNB has some deviations: it specifies that the man's arms and legs were swollen, that the man came to him, and that Jesus just "took" the man, not "took hold" of him. The NKJV specifically refers to dropsy, and adds that lawyers and Pharisees (i.e. plural) were present. The Greek *udrōpikos* can be specifically translated as dropsy, *epilabomenos* as take hold of, and *iasato* as heal or cure.

The single report reduces the reliability of this case and, although there were a number of witnesses, there was no mention of the disciples. Dr Major comments that dropsy, or oedema, can have several causes variously involving heart, liver, kidneys or nutritional deficiencies, but an instant cure for any of these is unlikely. If, therefore, this was instantaneous healing, it would have had to be a supernatural one. This is the third example of Sabbath healing so far and, although the GNB states that the man came to Jesus, this is not confirmed in the other versions or the Greek. Thus Jesus may again have deliberately selected a likely candidate to demonstrate his opposition to the rule that forbade any work on the Sabbath.

Verdict: If this story is accurate, an instant healing would have been supernatural in origin.

Severed ear

Although this healing is reported in Luke (22:50–51), the event, up to but *excluding* the healing, is included in John (18:10). Jesus was going to be arrested, and one of his followers cut off the right ear of a servant of the high priest. Jesus said "No more of this" and (in Luke) touched the man's ear and healed him. John adds that the servant's name was Malchus, and the person who wielded the sword was Peter. The GNB specifies that in Luke the followers were the disciples whilst the NKJV states "those around him"; otherwise the texts agree with NIV. The Greek *apheilen* means take away or cut off, *hapsamenos* means touch or take hold of and the word *iasato* is used for heal or cure as previously.

The credibility of this account suffers from the differences between Luke's version and that of John. The latter is the only one of them who could have been an eyewitness and he does not include the healing act. If the healing did in fact take place as Luke stated, an instantaneous restoration of a completely severed ear could not have occurred naturalistically, although a partly severed one might have appeared to be retained, especially if it had been held in place for a time. Alternately, there may be an element of allegory in this story relating to forgiving one's enemies.

Verdict: In view of its doubtful accuracy, an allegory is perhaps more likely than a supernatural healing.

Invalid man at Bethesda

Only John (5:1–15) reports this case. Disabled people used to lie in the colonnades around the pool of Bethesda in Jerusalem. When the water in the pool showed the appearance of being stirred, the first person to immerse him- or herself believed they would be cured. One man had been waiting for thirty-eight years, but said that there was nobody to help him into the pool so he had never been in first. Jesus asked him if he wanted to get well, then simply told the man to get up, pick up his mat and walk. He did so and was cured. This is another example of a healing on the Sabbath, and the Jewish leaders chastised the man for carrying his mat on that day, but Jesus had disappeared into the crowd by then.

The GNB uses "had been ill" instead of the NIV's "had been an invalid", and "got well" in place of "was cured", whilst the NKJV refers to an "infirmity" that was made well. The latter version includes verses 3b–4 that the others omit but mention in footnotes. This relates to the belief that an angel of the Lord would sometimes stir the water and the first to then enter it would be healed. The Greek version also excludes this passage from the main body of the text but likewise acknowledges its existence. It refers to the man in "his sickness" (*astheneia*) being made "healthy" (*hugiēs*).

Whilst John himself might have been a witness, and others, including some Pharisees, were involved, his is the only Gospel account. This time Jesus does not initiate an opportunity to make his point about doing good deeds on the Sabbath. There seems to be something rather unusual about a man being by the pool for as long thirty-eight years without being able to find anybody to help him be first into the water. No details are given of the man's illness other than the various general terms used in the different translations. If he had a conversion disorder that manifested in a form of paralysis, or maybe arthritis, then Jesus could have enacted a "faith" healing. Asking the man if he wanted to be made well could have given him confidence. However, the man may have been a professional beggar and malingerer, and Jesus intentionally or fortuitously "called his bluff."

Verdict: This is unlikely to have been a genuine healing, but an open verdict can be recorded if it was.

CHAPTER 10

THE FIRST THREE EXORCISMS

GRINDHEIM (2013)[1] NOTES THAT it is only in the NT that demons are described as occupying human beings, and that the authors are able to distinguish between sickness and demon occupation. The examples cited in this chapter and the next specifically relate to demon occupation rather than simply sickness involving disturbed behavior.

The man at Capernaum

There are six cases of exorcism recorded in the Gospels and this first example is paralleled in two of them. Mark (1:21–27) states that Jesus was with his disciples teaching in a synagogue on the Sabbath when a man possessed by an impure spirit shouted at him. The man asked Jesus what he wanted with them (the synagogue congregation), but added that he knew he was the Holy One of God. Jesus said "be quiet! . . . come out of him", and the spirit did so "with a shriek". Luke (4:31–36) added the word "demon" and, when Jesus commands it to come out, it threw the man down, but the demon came out without injuring him. The GNB uses the term "evil spirit" in Mark and "the spirit of an evil demon" in Luke, but otherwise the versions substantially agree. The NKJV prefers "unclean

---

1. *Demons Occupying Human Beings*, 24–25.

spirit", which "convulsed" the man when it left him (Mark) and "unclean demon" that threw the man in their midst on exit. The Greek version confirms the main facts: *pneumati akathartō* means unclean spirit, *exēlthen* means go forth or come out, *sparaxan* means convulse or throw a fit, *daimoniou* means demon or evil spirit, and *rhipsan* means throw, hurl, or cast out.

A general consideration of possible causes and symptoms of "demonic possession" will inform this and the similar cases that follow. Firstly there are various physical causes of at least some of the manifestations associated with this syndrome, such as drugs (especially hallucinogenic ones), high fever, epilepsy, malarial rigors or even bread made from flour contaminated with ergot – a mould containing psychotropic chemicals. More commonly, however, the cause will have a psychological origin, including bipolar disorder, where mood and behavior alternates between manic episodes and depression, and paranoia, with its delusions and belief that one is being persecuted. In some cultures today, for example Haiti, there is a belief in Voodoo and other possession states which, as Kaplan and Sadock (1981)[2] explain, involve the conviction that one can be involuntarily possessed by evil spirits. Because of this, chronic hysterical and psychosomatic symptoms may be induced, including epileptic seizures.

Mass hysteria, also known as mass psychogenic illness, typically begins when an individual is sick or hysterical during periods of stress, and can manifest as nausea, muscle weakness, fits, headaches and violent behavior. Those who are emotionally vulnerable and in close contact may then be "infected", leading to what appears to be an outbreak of an organic infectious disease for which no physical cause is evident. Waller (2009)[3] reviews such cases that have occurred over the last seven hundred years or so, starting with an outbreak of dancing mania along the River Rhine in 1374 that then spread through France and the Netherlands. In 1491 nuns in the Spanish Netherlands were plunged into states of frantic delirium that included sexual propositioning, and in 1518

2. *Voodoo and Other Possession States*, 660.

3. *Dancing Plagues and Mass Hysteria*, 644–47.

more dancing plagues commenced. Waller explains that cases such as these involved "dissociative trance" of which one symptom is loss of self-control, and that such epidemics usually took place in fearful and depressed communities.

Precipitating factors included severe flooding, famine and cold that caused despair or, in the case of the nuns, the requirements of extreme piety and austerity that led to a guilty longing for human intimacy. Because many were in the same situation, the mental breakdown of a few became contagious and quickly spread into an epidemic. There are modern examples too, with an outbreak of mass anxiety hysteria at a school in Blackburn, UK in 1965 where 141 pupils were afflicted with symptoms of dizziness, spasms and breath shortage, and one of mass motor hysteria at a school near Lake Tanganyika, where pupils developed a compulsion to laugh and cry. A famous case, first reported in 1994 at Toronto Airport Vineyard Church in Canada, became known as the "Toronto Blessing", with many people exhibiting uncontrollable laughter, shaking, shouting and falling that may last for several days.

The cultural context is therefore important when considering cases of possession, and the people in Jesus' time accepted the existence of evil spirits that could cause illness, and that this could occur, inter alia, through sinning or the guilt associated with the belief that they had done so (see also "Eyewitness expectations" vide supra). In this first example, the man concerned appeared to be anxious and stressed. Whilst recognizing that Jesus was "the Holy One of God" and presumably had awesome powers, the man was clearly apprehensive of him. However, Jesus acted with authority and ordered the spirit to depart. If the man believed that Jesus did have divine powers, he could have accepted that he had been exorcised of the evil spirit.

While Jesus no doubt acted with compassion in exorcising the man, he would also have been glad to end the noisy disruption to his teaching and to avoid what might have been an oblique challenge to his credibility. This is yet another Sabbath healing, although on this occasion Jesus was not challenged for it and did not need to defend himself.

Verdict: Whilst a supernaturalistic intervention involving a physical condition can not be totally excluded, for this example of exorcism, a psychological condition that was cured by a psychological or "faith" intervention is probably the most likely explanation.

Demons transferred to pigs

This case is reported in each of the Synoptic Gospels. Matthew (8:28–34) refers to two fierce demoniacs, who lived in tombs in the region of the Gadarenes. They shouted at Jesus, calling him "Son of God", asking him what he wanted of them, and if he had come to "torment them before the time". Jesus commanded the demons to go, and they entered a passing herd of pigs that then rushed into the sea and were drowned. Mark (5:1–20) adds much more detail, but only mentions one man, called Legion, who had an unclean spirit. He shouted and self-harmed day and night, even though people had, unsuccessfully, tried to constrain him with chains. Jesus had already commanded the unclean spirits to come out but the man begged Jesus not to send him out of the country. The spirits asked to be transferred to the swine; Jesus agreed, the spirits departed and entered about 2,000 pigs; and the man was cured. Luke (8:26–39) also only refers to one man, called Legion, noting that he was from the city but did not wear any clothes. The "demons" begged Jesus not to send them back into the "abyss", and the pigs drowned in the "lake".

In Matthew's version, the GNB prefers "punish us" to "torment us", "burial caves" to "tombs", and that the pigs ended up in the "lake" rather than the "sea". Mark's version has the man "screaming" at Jesus rather than "shouted", and both this and Luke's version translate the man's name as "Mob" not "Legion". The NKJV generally parallels the terminology of the NIV. The Greek account translates *mnēmeiōn* as tomb or grave, *basanisai* as afflict, torment, or harass, *Legiōn* as legion, army, or many, *chōras* as territory, district, or region, and *abusson* as bottomless pit or abyss. The GNB is the only version among several consulted that names the man "Mob". Whilst "Legion" was meant to signify the many

53

demons with which the man was afflicted, rather than his actual name, and, as "Mob" has similar connotations, using the latter term seems unnecessary.

This example gains credibility and reliability from there being parallel accounts that between them provide much detail but, as with the fourth case of blindness (Matt 20:29–34 et al., vide supra) the first evangelist cites two afflicted demonics, whereas the other two cite just one. Matthew was the only one of the three writers who could have been an eye-witness, so the others would have relied on second-hand accounts. The story includes the information that people in the nearby town saw that the man/men was/were now acting normally. The circumstances bear some resemblance to the first example of exorcism, with the possessed man/men being agitated and anxious. This was not helped by the presence of Jesus who was seen as someone with divine powers that could be used against him/them, including banishment. Again Jesus addressed the demons with a voice of authority, and the exorcism took place. The fact that the pigs then became possessed is difficult to explain rationally, unless they were just frightened by all the commotion and shouting and, following the herd instinct, galloped away. Whether or not this aspect of the story is exaggerated, or had become at least partly fanciful with the passage of time before being written down, is uncertain.

A range of potential naturalistic causes for a possessed condition was reviewed in the general discussion of the first exorcism example and, for this second case, these could include a bipolar disorder that had severe manic episodes, or hysteria brought on by a situation of religious uncertainty and the knowledge that a person with divine powers was touring the country. As in the first case, Jesus would have acted from compassion.

Verdict: The likelihood of this exorcism being accomplished through naturalistic means rules out the certainty of a supernaturalistic intervention.

The man unable to speak

This case is recorded only by Matthew (9:32–34). The account is short, stating simply that a demon-possessed man who was unable to talk was brought to Jesus. When the demon had been driven out, the man spoke. However, a Pharisee said that it was the prince of demons who had given Jesus the power to drive out demons. The GNB prefers "chief" of demons, and the NKJV "ruler". The Greek retains the same word as before for "demon", and uses *archonti* as prince or ruler, and *ekballei* meaning to throw out or expel.

Whilst Matthew could have been an eye-witness, and others were also present, including at least one Pharisee, this is just a single account that is very short on detail. It is not stated how long the person had been possessed, nor how Jesus conducted the exorcism. The story describes the affliction as a demon possession rather than a simple case of dumbness, but there is no mention of violent behavior. Temporary dumbness is one of the many manifestations of hysterical neurosis or conversion disorder, precipitated by factors such as stress, fear, guilt or anxiety. Jesus was continuing to act from compassion and could have forgiven the man his sins or commanded the demon to depart.

Verdict: This case probably does have a naturalistic explanation, and thus a supernaturalistic one seems unlikely.

CHAPTER 11

THE REMAINING THREE
EXORCISMS

Demon-possessed daughter

BOTH MATTHEW (15:21–28) AND Mark (7:24–30) report this example. In the former Gospel, a Canaanite woman kept shouting at Jesus begging him to go and heal her daughter who was being tormented by a demon. At first he resisted, but the woman demonstrated great faith. Jesus said that because of this her daughter would be healed and, when the woman arrived home, she found that this was so. Mark's version is similar, but the woman was not said to be shouting, and the demon is at first referred to as an unclean spirit. The woman is described as a Gentile of Syro-Phoenician origin, hence a non-Jew and a foreigner. The GNB adds that the daughter was said to be in a "terrible condition" (Matthew) and first describes the demon as an "evil spirit" (Mark). The NKJV prefers "severely" possessed and "unclean spirit". The Greek version is again consistent with the words used previously for "demon" and "unclean spirit", and favors *iathē* for healed or cured.

The two parallel versions and the presence of at least some disciples as witnesses for the encounter between Jesus and the woman aid the reliability and accuracy of this account, but no mention is made of witnesses to the daughter's cure. Likewise, no details are given of the onset and duration of the possession. This is another example of a cure without Jesus actually seeing the patient, as was reported for the paralyzed centurion's servant (Matt 8:5–13) and the official's son with fever (John 4:46–54). The actual medical condition is therefore uncertain, and there may have been an organic cause as well as one of the recognized psychological syndromes. In view of the mother's agitation, it is possible that the onset was sudden and that an equally sudden, naturalistic healing occurred.

Although Jesus uncharacteristically seems to treat the woman harshly at first (possibly because she was a foreigner and non-Jew?), he ultimately responded positively to her faith. Knowing this, the woman would have returned home in an optimistic frame of mind and would have regarded any sign of improvement in her daughter's condition positively.

Verdict: Whilst a supernaturalistic intervention remains possible, a naturalistic cure is probably more likely.

The boy with a demon

Each of the Synoptic Gospels reports this incident. Matthew (17:14–20) states that a man knelt before Jesus and told him that his son was an epileptic who suffered terribly. The man had already asked the disciples to heal the boy, but they had failed to do so. Jesus asked for the boy to be brought to him; he cast the demon out and the boy was cured instantly. Mark's (9:14–29) version provides a surprising amount of additional medical detail. The affliction is described as a spirit that renders the boy dumb and dashes him down with foaming mouth, grinding teeth and rigidity. Mark adds that the boy then suffered another convulsion in front of Jesus. In answer to a question, the father said that the affliction originated in childhood. The father asked for pity and declared his faith. Jesus commanded the spirit to depart and it did so but created a terrible convulsion in the process, leaving the boy like a corpse. Jesus, however, lifted him up. Despite being regarded as a physician, Luke's (9:37–43) version is the shortest of the three, adding only that the boy was an only child, and that he suffered a convulsion on the way to Jesus, rather than after he had arrived .

In Mark's account, the GNB adds that Jesus commanded the "deaf and dumb spirit" to come out and, in Luke's account, that Jesus was with three disciples (Peter, James and John, as cited in the preceding pericope), but otherwise it parallels the NIV version. The NKJV is similar but states that the boy was cured "from that very hour" rather than "instantly" (Matthew). The Greek words for demon, unclean spirit, rebuked, and healed are as before, although *etherapeuthē* is used for healed in Matthew. *Selēniazetai* is used for mentally out of control or lunatic (although it is also used for epileptic), *pneuma alalon* for mute spirit and *sunesparaxen* for convulse or having a fit.

The many witnesses, the parallel accounts and the combined detail support the reliability and accuracy of this incident. In fact, so explicit are the symptoms that Dr Major states that a modern-day medical diagnosis of tonic-clonic seizure with post-ictal phase is possible, rather than demonic possession. Tonic-clonic seizure is commonly, but not exclusively, associated with epilepsy, and is typified by a loss-of-consciousness phase sometimes accompanied by moans or screams, followed by a phase of convulsions and stiffness, and concluding with a period of altered state of consciousness and confusion. Today this condition is usually treated, but not cured, with drug therapy, electrical stimulation of the brain, or surgery. Certain life-style and dietary changes have also been known to help relieve the symptoms.

If Jesus effected a permanent cure, then this would have been a supernatural healing. Because the condition is manifested by discrete episodes of the syndrome, what is described in the story as a cure might simply have been the end of a particular attack. As with many of the biblical stories of healings there was, understandably, no long-term follow-up to confirm that the cure was permanent.

Verdict: Without further evidence, there must be some doubt that a healing took place at all. If it did, then it might just have been a temporary, naturalistic one helped by Jesus' compassion.

Blind and mute demonic man

This incident is reported in each of the first three Gospels, although very briefly. According to Matthew (12:22–24), people from the crowds who were following Jesus brought to him a blind and mute demonic, and he cured him. The Pharisees present accused Jesus of using the power of Beelzebul, the ruler of the demons, to do this (see also third example: "the man unable to speak"). Mark (3:19–22) mentions no specific incident, but only that the scribes from Jerusalem said that Jesus must have Beelzebul's power to be able to cast out demons. Luke (11:14–16) states that Jesus was casting out a mute demon (no mention of the man being blind) and the afflicted then spoke. This time it is some of the crowd who accuse Jesus of using Beelzebul's power.

The GNB and NKJV versions are very similar, but the former prefers "chief" of the demons to "ruler" in Mark and Luke. The Greek translation uses the same words as before for demon and healed/cured (Matthew) and has *tuphlos* for blind; *kōphos* for mute or incapable of speech, and *ekballei* for expel or drive out.

Although there are parallel, though somewhat different, accounts and many witnesses for this example, there is very little detail to help the evaluation. The cause is again attributed to a demon, but the named symptoms are restricted to blindness and dumbness (Matthew) or just blindness (Luke), and no origin or duration of the condition is given. Likewise no details are provided of the procedure Jesus used for the healing. The blindness and dumbness might have had a psychosomatic origin, possibly a fairly recent conversion disorder brought on by stress, fear or deprivation. This would respond to a naturalistic or "faith" cure by a compassionate healer. However, this is yet another example of Jesus defying convention, either by healing on the Sabbath or by carrying out acts that were regarded as the prerogative of the devil. Are these healing reports intentionally contrived to emphasize this, even at the expense of the accuracy of the actual healings?

Verdict: In the absence of further details, the most likely explanation is a naturalistic healing.

CHAPTER 12

RAISING OF THE DEAD

The widow's son

THERE ARE THREE EXAMPLES of raising the dead in the Gospels, the first being reported only by Luke (7:11–17). Jesus was visiting the town of Nain and saw a dead man being carried, presumably for burial. It was the only son of a widow. Jesus was filled with compassion, touched the bier, and commanded the young man to get up. The man sat up and began to talk. There were many witnesses, including the disciples. The GNB specifically adds that it was a funeral procession and prefers "coffin" to "bier", whilst the NKJV also states "coffin" and adds that it was open. The Greek version does not include the words "funeral procession", but it does translate *sorou* as coffin or an open bier to carry people for burial. "Have died" is the translation of *tethnēkōs*, and "awake or arouse" is the meaning of *egerthēti*.

This example gains from there being many witnesses but there are no parallel accounts. Whether or not this was a supernatural intervention rests on a lack of certainty that the young man was actually dead, and we are not given any information about the cause of "death" or how recently it had occurred. Jewish burials were by tradition carried out shortly after death, and preferably on the same day. Although Deuteronomy 21:23 refers to criminals having to be buried on the same day and the body not kept overnight, this was also the usual custom with ordinary people. This might have been because of the hazards associated with decomposition, but it was also considered a praiseworthy act.[1]

Catalepsy is a condition that can mimic the appearance of a person being dead. It is a nervous disorder characterized by muscular rigidity and fixed posture regardless of external stimuli ("waxy flexibility"). There is also a slowing of bodily functions including breathing. Kaplan and Sadock (1981)[2] state that this syndrome is characteristic of catatonic schizophrenia and it can also be induced by hypnotic suggestion. Other precipitating conditions can include Parkinson's disease, extreme emotional shock or trauma, and epilepsy (see also "Boy with a demon" exorcism, vide supra) where the rigidity of the post-ictal phase of a seizure can resemble death). Throughout history there have been anecdotal reports of people being buried alive due to catalepsy being mistaken for death, and the speed with which Jewish burials take place can only increase the likelihood of this occurring. A similar and possibly related condition is narcolepsy, characterized by an abnormal tendency to sleep during the day, along with the likelihood of sudden paralysis (Kaplan & Sadock, 1981)[3].

The Gospels only report the three cases of raising the dead, and it may be that Jesus was skilled, or divinely guided, toward selecting cases where he suspected the patient might still be alive but in a cataleptic state. There is no mention of Jesus being asked to perform this miracle, only that he acted out of compassion, maybe after noticing clues that the man might not actually have been dead. Although medication may be prescribed as treatment for such cases today, in many instances the patient recovers naturally and most effort is devoted to helping remedy the underlying cause.

Verdict: Because a naturalistic explanation is possible for this instance of raising the dead, the premise that it was a supernatural intervention is not strongly supported.

---

1. *jewishencyclopedia.com*
2. *Disturbances in Aspects of Motor Behavior*, 263–64.
3. *Conditions Producing Chiefly Excessive Sleepiness*, 676–80.

Jairus' daughter

This case is well documented in each of the Synoptic Gospels. Matthew (9:18, 23–26) states that a synagogue leader came to Jesus and told him that his daughter had just died but that, if he went and laid his hands on her, she would live. Jesus went with his disciples to the house and said that the girl was just sleeping. He then took her by the hand and she got up. Mark (5:21–43) names the man as Jairus, and his account differs by having the man say that his daughter was "on the point" of death but, before Jesus and his disciples arrived at the house, people told them that the girl had died. Jesus told the man not to fear but to believe, and entered the house together with the parents and Peter, James and John. Jesus took the girl, described as being about twelve years old, by the hand and told her to get up, which she did and started to walk about. Luke (8:40–56) closely parallels Mark but adds that "her spirit returned" and, significantly, that Jesus told the parents to give the child something to eat.

The GNB agrees with the NIV version except it refers to Jairus as a "Jewish official" instead of a "synagogue leader" (Matthew), and that her "life" rather than "spirit" returned (Luke). The NKJV simply calls Jairus a "ruler" (Matthew) or "one of the rulers of the synagogue" (Mark, similar in Luke) and that the girl "arose" (all three Gospels) instead of "got up". In Matthew, the Greek *eteleutēsen* means came to an end or died, and *ēgerthē* means awakened or arose; in Mark *eschatōs* means at the point of death, *apethane* means to die or suffer death, *kratēsas* means to take hold 'forcibly', *egeirai* means cause to stand up or arise, and *phagein* means to eat or have a meal; whilst in Luke *epestrepse to enema* means her spirit returned.

The reliability of this story gains from the parallel accounts and combined details, with several disciples being witnesses although none of them were the Synoptic Gospel writers. The versions do, however, differ in whether the girl was already dead when Jairus approached Jesus, or died just before Jesus arrived at the house. Either way, the death appears to have been very recent, and Jairus had faith that Jesus could raise her. Although, as reviewed in the discussion of the first case of raising the dead (vide supra), there is a range of medical or psychological conditions that can mimic death, Dr Major thinks that in this case it could have been hypoglycemia, a coma brought on by a low blood sugar level. One cause of this is insulinoma, a benign pancreatic tumor, whilst today it could be due to insulin administered to a diabetic who then does not take in nourishment. A low blood sugar level can also be the result of anorexic fasting.

There are no details of the girl experiencing any similar episodes before. As Jairus was a synagogue leader, it is possible that Jesus knew him and that his daughter suffered from spasmodic attacks, although perhaps of less severity than the present one. The symptoms of what is now called diabetes were known in those times, but not its cause. Jesus might have been familiar with the syndrome, plus the fact that eating could lead to recovery from the coma: an important point that is added only in Luke's version. The Greek word *kratēsas* used in Mark's story indicates that Jesus had to firmly grasp the girl's hand to raise her up, and that she was then sufficiently recovered to be able to eat. This would have the effect of raising her blood sugar level. However, it is appreciated that this is just speculation.

Verdict: If the child was indeed suffering from a hyperglycemic coma, Jesus could have used natural rather than supernatural means to affect what would have appeared to the witnesses as a raising from the dead.

The raising of Lazarus

This is only reported in John's Gospel (11:1–45), and it is a long account commencing with a statement that Jesus' friend Lazarus, the brother of Martha and Mary, was ill, and that a message had been sent to Jesus informing him of this. Jesus replied that the illness would not end in death, and delayed going to visit Lazarus for two days. Jesus told the disciples that Lazarus was asleep—meaning that he had died and that he, Jesus, would go and wake him up. When the party arrived, they found that Lazarus had been lying in his tomb for four days. First Martha and then Mary gently chastised Jesus, saying that their brother would not have died if he had been there, but Jesus gave them a short homily about how those who believed in him would live. Nevertheless Jesus was deeply moved and wept. When the party arrived at the tomb, he asked for the stone to be rolled away, prayed heavenwards, and called out to Lazarus to come out. Lazarus did so, still covered in the burial bandages.

The GNB and NKJV closely agree, apart from their individual linguistic styles. The Greek translations of the key words are unambiguous: *kekoimētai* means fall asleep or, figuratively, dying, *exupnisō* means wake up or, figuratively, become alive again, *mnēmeiō* means tomb or grave, *deuro exō* means come here, outside, *tethnekōs* means having died, and *dedemenos* means bind or wrap up, as in a burial.

Whilst this example of Jesus raising the dead is only described in one Gospel, there are witnesses, possibly including John himself. There is much detail in the complete story, although that concerning the actual raising is limited to Jesus just calling Lazarus to come out of the tomb. Jesus obviously knew Lazarus well, and it is possible he was aware that his friend could have had one of the medical conditions mentioned earlier that result in temporary catatonic trances or comas. This might explain why Jesus did not find it necessary to rush straight to Lazarus when he heard his friend was ill. If this were indeed the case, this is another example of Jesus exhibiting a remarkable medical knowledge of both physical and psychological illnesses, but it also might confirm that he restricted his healings, exorcisms and raisings to examples he knew would respond to naturalistic cures.

The fact that this pericope included more than one short homily suggests that John might have included the story more for the message than the raising itself, or even that the raising was purely symbolic. In verse four Jesus says that Lazarus's illness will not result in death, but it (the illness) is for God's glory so that his son may be glorified through it. In verse ten Jesus tells the disciples that people stumble when they walk at night because they have no light. Then in verse twenty-five Jesus said to Martha that he is the resurrection and the life, and that one who believes in him will live even though they die. Martha responds that she believes that Jesus is the Messiah, the Son of God. In verse forty, at the tomb, Jesus reminds Martha that, if she believed, she would see the glory of God.

Verdict: There are three possibilities: it is a case of supernaturalistic intervention with someone who was really dead, a naturalistic recovery of someone who was not really dead, or it is partly or wholly a symbolic story to emphasize the glory and compassion of Jesus as the Son of God.

CHAPTER 13

NATURE: CHANGING WATER INTO WINE; THE FIRST CATCH OF FISH

THERE ARE NINE EXAMPLES of miracles where it appears that the laws of nature have been contravened. Unlike the examples discussed so far, the nature miracles cannot be explained by reference to medical or psychological conditions, except perhaps for the hypothetical possibility of delusions or hypnosis. A number of scholars have offered opinions on what could have happened in the case of these miracles, and these will be included in the analyses that follow.

Changing water into wine

Only John (2:1–11) reports this miracle. Jesus, His mother and disciples were invited to a wedding. Mary told Jesus that the wine had run out, but he asked her why she had involved him and said that his hour had not yet come. Nevertheless, Jesus told the servants to fill six large stone jars with water, and then take some of the liquid to the banquet master. The master tasted it— it had turned into wine—and proclaimed that usually the best wine was served first, but this time the best had been saved until last. John adds that this was the first of the signs that revealed Jesus' glory, and that the disciples believed in him. The GNB is substantially the same, except that Jesus more specifically asks Mary not to tell him what to do, and that this was Jesus' first "miracle" (cf. "sign"). The NKJV phrases Jesus' statement to his mother "What does your concern have to do with me?", but retains "signs".

The Greek confirms the key aspects of this story: *ti emoi kai-soi* means your concern is not mine, and *hudōr oinon gegenēmenon* means water came to be wine. Whilst this miracle is only reported in one Gospel, John could himself have been an eyewitness. Others were also present but, apart from the servants who filled the jars, not all of them were aware of what actually happened. If this were a genuine supernatural intervention, it would have involved manipulation of the laws of nature by which means physical matter had been instantly transmuted. Whilst this cannot be excluded, the principle on which the present investigation is based is to see if the evidence for an alternative premise negates the certainty of the original one (i.e. that it was a supernatural event).

Trench (1850)[1] thought that the wine might have been created by a speeding up of the natural fermentation process and thus it would not have been a contravention of the laws of nature as such. He did not, however, exclude the possibility of the story being an allegory of events to come, which would agree with Richards's (1975)[2] view that the future Kingdom of God was being likened to the joy of a wedding, and that the wine was a symbol of the longed-for joys of the future age. Blomberg (1984)[3] takes this further, suggesting that the old water of Judaism was converted into the new wine of Christianity, and that the final wedding feast between God and the people had begun.

---

1. *The Water Made Wine*, 95–114.

2. *Water into Wine*, 30–38.

3. *New Testament Miracles and Higher Criticism: Climbing the Slippery Slope*; 425–38.

Another allegorical possibility is pointed out by Grindheim (2013)[4] when he reminds us that wine was known to be a symbol of God's wisdom, as evidenced by the quotation in Proverbs (9:1–5) "She [wisdom] says . . . 'Come, eat my food and drink the wine I have mixed.'" Such notions of allegory seem to be popular among scholars, for example Blackburn (1992)[5] doubts that reports of miracles are based on actual reminiscence, suggesting instead that they relate to the coming of the Kingdom and promote Jesus as God's eschatological agent. He adds later (Blackburn, 2011)[6] that the nature miracles are less paralleled and witnessed than are the healing types, and are not supported by dominical sayings; he wonders if they were created by early Christians.

To deny that this miracle actually occurred as described would be to doubt the eyewitness reports. Keener (2011)[7], with specific reference to this miracle, defends such testimony but does concede that it is conditioned by the observer's interpretations. As was discussed earlier, other factors can also influence eyewitness testimony and the accuracy of recollections, especially after the passage of time, and useful details might have been lost.

Verdict: The explanation remains inconclusive: it may have been a supernatural intervention overriding the accepted laws of nature, or an allegorical story about Jesus' role as the source of wisdom, or even a simple case of someone bringing new wine to the party unobserved by the Gospel writer.

First miraculous catch of fish

This is only reported by Luke (5:1–11). Jesus had been preaching from a boat, and then he asked Simon Peter to go into deeper water and cast the nets. The disciple did so but said that he had not caught anything all night. The nets were then filled with so many

4. *Johannine Christology*, 115–6.

5. *Miracles and Miracle Stories*, 549–60.

6. *The Miracles of Jesus in History*, 116–20.

7. *Hume on Testimony*, 143–47.

fish that they risked breaking, and another boat had to be called to help safely land them. Jesus told Simon Peter that he would make him a fisher of men, and then this disciple, along with his partners James and John, left everything and followed Jesus. The GNB is similar but Jesus is reported to have asked Simon Peter "and his partners" to cast the nets (not specifically in deeper water). The NKJV retains the request to just the one disciple. The Greek translation contains no ambiguities: *chalasate* means let down or lower (the nets), and *anthrōpous esē zōgrōn* means (you will) catch or attract ordinary men (i.e. be fishers of men).

This account contains useful details about the boats and the catch that lend it an air of credibility, but it was not written by an actual eyewitness and is not paralleled in the other Gospels. The good catch of fish when nothing was caught overnight could have been a natural event that was divinely brought about (Trench, 1850)[8], or was due to Jesus' superior knowledge of where and when fish tend to congregate (Erickson, 1985)[9]. Trench also sees a symbolic meaning relating to "fishers of men": when the "fisher" casts his net he is not sure what sort of "fish" will enter it. This concurs with Blomberg's (1984)[10] view that the nature miracles in particular, including the present example, have a symbolic character that precludes objections to their historicity, and Wright's (1927)[11] comment that they reveal Jesus' presence in nature and upon the organic world. As suggested by Keener (2011)[12], however, this and other nature miracles may contain embellishments of real events, or describe subjective experiences of the disciples.

Verdict: The evidence for this miracle being a supernatural event is not strong, and it was most likely either a natural event initiated by Jesus, or a symbolic story relating to Simon Peter being made a "fisher of men".

8. *The First Miraculous Draft of Fishes*, 125–41.

9. *Providence and Miracles*, 406–10.

10. *New Testament Miracles and Higher Criticism: Climbing the Slippery Slope*; 425–38.

11. *Miracles*, 186–91.

12. *Limits of Naturalistic Explanations*, 580–81.

CHAPTER 14

NATURE: CALMING THE STORM; FEEDING THE FIVE THOUSAND

Calming the storm

EACH OF THE SYNOPTIC Gospels reports this example. Matthew (8: 23–27) states that Jesus and his disciples were crossing the lake when a windstorm arose that was swamping the boat. Jesus was asleep but the disciples woke him and asked him to save them. Jesus asked them why they were afraid, and accused them of having little faith. He then rebuked the wind and the sea, and there was a dead calm. The disciples were amazed. Mark's version (4:35–41) adds the details that Jesus was sleeping in the stern on a cushion, and that he rebuked the wind and said to the sea "peace! Be still!" But he did this first before chastising the disciples. Luke's (8:22–25) account concurs that the elements were rebuked before the faith of the disciples was questioned.

The GNB as usual modernizes some of the phrases, such as the boat was in "danger of sinking" instead of "being swamped", and "we are about to die" rather than "perishing" (Matthew); "waves . . . spill over the boat" versus "beat into the boat", and Jesus asleep with "his head on a pillow" instead of "on a cushion" (Mark); and "gave an order to the wind" rather than "rebuked" it (Luke). The NKJV calls the storm a "tempest" and that the boat was "covered with waves" (cf. "swamped") (Matthew). In Mark "windstorm" is retained, but the boat was "filling" (with water) rather than "being swamped" and the calm was "great" rather then "dead". The disciples are described as being in "jeopardy" instead of "danger" in Luke.

The Greek translation confirms the basic facts: *seismos megas* means great storm, *kaluptesthai* means cover up (i.e. with waves), *epetimēoen* means rebuke or admonish, *galēnē* means calm or stillness, *apollumetha* means pass away or perish, *lailaps* means furious gust of wind, *deiloi* means timid, fearful, or cowardly, and *proskephalaion* means boat cushion. It is interesting that the last of these words specifically indicates a cushion fitted to a boat, rather than the pillow preferred by the GNB, and there is no mention in the Greek of Jesus' head being on a pillow. The alternative translations generally account for the variations in the English versions.

The existence of three similar parallel versions, plus the presence of at least some of the disciples—one of whom might have been a Gospel writer— provides reliability and accuracy for this event. As pointed out by Keener (2011)[1], other instances of having control over the waters appear in the OT, for example Moses parting the Red Sea (Exod 14:21) and Joshua stopping the Jordan flowing (Josh 3:13–16). Indeed, the pious Israelites believed the hand of God was present in nature; miracles belonged to the natural concept of God's working and were accepted as such (Ropes, 1910)[2].

Whilst this miracle could have been an example of God directly manipulating the natural order (Twelftree, 2011)[3], Trench (1850)[4] wonders why Jesus rebuked the disciples for having little faith when they could not have known that he would save them, especially when he was asleep. He suggests that the point of the story could relate to people not having faith and letting Jesus sleep in their hearts. A similar symbolic interpretation is reflected in

1. *Limits of Ancient Analogies*, 581–87.

2. *Some Aspects of New Testament Miracles*, 482–99.

3. *Fundamental Issues*, 3–6.

4. *The Stilling of the Tempest*, 142–49.

Blomberg's (1984)[5] suggestion that the story could depict the protection that Jesus affords the church through the storms of life, and that this power over nature mirrors the divine sovereignty of God himself.

Verdict: Whilst this miracle can be explained as a natural event, whether or not due to divine intervention, there is support for the notion that it was not meant to be taken literally but was intended to illustrate Jesus' role and the need to have faith in him.

Feeding the five thousand

This is the only one of the thirty-five miracles considered here that are reported in all four Gospels. Matthew (14:13–21) describes how a great crowd had followed Jesus and the disciples to a deserted place. It was evening and the disciples suggested to Jesus that he send the crowds away to the surrounding villages to buy food, but he responded by telling *them* to provide some food. They only had five loaves and two fish, but Jesus took them, blessed the loaves, broke them and gave them to the disciples to distribute (there is no further mention of the fish). Everyone ate their fill, and twelve baskets of broken pieces were left over. There were about five thousand men, plus women and children. Mark (6:30–44) provides additional details. The disciples said that it would cost two hundred denarii to buy enough bread. In this account, the people were asked to sit in groups of one hundred and fifty, and the fish were distributed as well as the bread.

Luke's (9:10–17) version is a similar but shorter version to that of Mark. John (6:1–15) adds that it was near the time of the Jewish Passover Festival, and that it was Jesus who asked Philip where they could buy bread, but he did this only to test him. Philip responded that it would take over half a year's wages to let everyone have a bite. Andrew then said that a boy had the loaves, adding that they were barley, and the fish. Jesus took them, gave thanks, and distributed them to the seated people.

5. *New Testament Miracles and Higher Criticism: Climbing the Slippery Slope*, 425–38.

The GNB versions are similar, with only minor deviations such as "nearby farms and villages" instead of "surrounding country and villages" (Mark and Luke); "silver coins" instead of "denarii", and "thanked God" instead of "blessed" (Mark); and "have even a little" instead of "have a bite" (John). In the NKJV the crowds are "commanded" to sit down rather than "ordered" (Matthew); the day "began to wear away" instead of "was drawing to a close" (Luke); and "two hundred denarii" instead of "half a year's wages" (John).

The Greek version generally confirms the alternative translations: *keleusas* means command, order or direct; *echortasthēsan* means feed, satisfy, or fill up; *kophinous* means basket, especially the wicker type for food; *agrous* means field, country, or rural area (i.e. not specifically "farm" as in the GNB, even though this may be implied); *eulogēsen* means give thanks or bless; *klinein* means be about to end (i.e. the day); and *brachu* means a little or a small amount. There is, however, no direct justification for the NIV's unique rendering of *diakosiōn dēnariōn* (two hundred denarius or silver coins) as "more than half a year's wages".

There is a surprising amount of parallel information concerning this miracle which provides much detail when combined. The reliability of the story is supported by the presence of all or many of the disciples, not to mention the large number of people who partook of the food. The debating point is thus limited to whether or not food was miraculously multiplied as stated. Just as stilling the storm (vide supra) is not the only biblical example of control over the waters, the present miracle is one of several relating to feeding (Blackburn, 2011)[6]. God provides manna and quail for the Israelites (Exod 16:4–36), multiplies olive oil (2 Kgs 4:2–6), Elisha feeds a group of prophets with barley bread (2 Kgs 4:42–44), and a widow feeds Elijah with bread made from flour and oil that does not run out (1 Kgs 17:12–16). Trench (1850)[7] opines that the present example does not involve the speeding up of a natural process that he thought might, for example, explain the water becoming wine (vide supra) and so it must be a case of supernatural multiplying.

6. *The Miracles of Jesus*, 113–30.
7. *The Miraculous Feeding of Five Thousand*, 261–73.

Most scholars, however, are more skeptical and believe that there are either obvious simple or allegorical interpretations. Blomberg (1984)[8] cites the view that this story might be meant to indicate that Jesus, who feeds the people now in token of the impending Kingdom and the Messianic Feast, will never fail to feed the faithful. Similarly, Montefiore (2005)[9] suggests a possible mythical or symbolic explanation for this and other examples of "feeding" miracles, in that these may be cases of spiritual rather than physical feeding. Richards (1975)[10] also speculates on a symbolic meaning: that a yearning for union with God is being likened to the hunger of starving men, and that God's Kingdom is being compared with a banquet. He also offers two possible simple explanations: firstly of a vast exaggeration in the crowd numbers and, secondly, that Jesus shared his own food and others then followed suit.

Ropes (1910)[11] raises the possibility that stories such as this may have been transformed in the telling. In similar vein, Keener (2011)[12] comments as he did in the case of feeding the five thousand, raising the possibility of such food multiplication being an embellishment of a real event, although it may also have been a subjective rather than an objective experience of the disciples. Doubt that any such event actually took place is voiced by Blackburn (2011)[13] when he wonders whether this story was created by the early Christians, based on Elisha's multiplication of loaves (vide supra).

Verdict: This event must have been meaningful to the disciples to generate four different accounts. It has to be either a genuine supernatural event where the laws of nature were bypassed and food was multiplied, a case of more food becoming available once the sharing had been encouraged or, as many commentators have suggested, a symbolic reference to spiritual feeding.

8. *New Testament Miracles and Higher Criticism: Climbing the Slippery Slope*, 425–38.

9. *The Feeding of the Multitudes*, 77–86.

10. *Food in the Desert*, 45–59.

11. *Some Aspects of New Testament Miracles*, 482–99.

12. *Limits of Naturalistic Explanations*, 580–1.

13. *The Miracles of Jesus*, 113–30.

CHAPTER 15

NATURE: JESUS WALKS ON WATER; FEEDING THE FOUR THOUSAND

Jesus walks on water

THIS IS DESCRIBED IN three out of the four Gospels, and is the only example of a miraculous act involving Jesus himself to be included in the present investigation. Matthew (14:22–33) reports that, after telling the disciples to get into the boat and go on ahead of him, Jesus went to pray alone up a mountain near the lake, and that the disciples in the boat were far from land and were in a head wind being battered by the waves. Early the following morning Jesus walked on the lake toward them, but the disciples thought it was a ghost. When Jesus confirmed it was he, Peter tried to walk on the water toward him but started to sink. He cried out to Jesus to save him and Jesus caught him, but rebuked him for having little faith. When Jesus got into the boat, the wind ceased. The disciples then said that Jesus was truly the Son of God. Mark's (6:45–52) version omits the passage about Peter, but states that Jesus walked on the sea and intended to pass by the boat, but the disciples cried out in fear and Jesus then reassured them and joined them in the boat.

In this description there is no mention of the disciples saying that Jesus was the Son of God, but the passage does state that they had not understood the loaves (presumably a reference to the miracle of the feeding of the five thousand). John (6:16–21) states that the disciples set off in the boat for Capernaum without Jesus, and that the sea was rough. After they had rowed three or four miles, they saw Jesus walking on the water toward them, and they were frightened. Jesus reassured them and got into the boat. They immediately reached their destination, but there is no specific mention of calming the storm. The GNB specifies that it was between three and six o'clock in the morning, instead of "early morning" (Matthew and Mark), and states that the disciples had not understood the real meaning of the "feeding of the five thousand" rather than the "loaves" (Mark).

In the NKJV, "the fourth watch of the night" is used instead of "early morning" (Matthew and Mark), but otherwise the three versions essentially agree. The Greek version confirms the key points: *tetartē de phulakē* means the fourth watch; *epi tēn thalassan* means on the sea or lake; *peripatōn* means walk or go along; and *tois artois* means the bread or loaves. The GNB's transcribing "fourth watch" as "between three and six o'clock" may be a helpful clarification but it is not a literal rendition.

The experience described in the three versions provides good confirmation that an event took place that was very frightening for the disciples, who perhaps included two of the Gospel writers themselves. There are, however, some indications that suggest the main message may be symbolic, two of which were noted by Trench (1850)[1]. Firstly, as Mark's version states, Jesus was going to walk right passed the boat until the disciples called out in fear and he then joined them. Secondly, Peter is mentioned in Matthew's story as wanting to join Jesus but he lost faith and starting to sink, crying out to Jesus to save him, which he did. In both these versions it is stated that the wind ceased once Jesus was present. Thus it could be that, when we lose faith, are in danger, and see Jesus neglecting us, we have to call out to him to be saved and then all is calm.

1. *The Walking on the Sea*, 274–86.

Richards (1975)[2] also sees this story as symbolic, with the sea representing the chaotic and hostile elements that God has to overcome. One who walks on the sea is its master, and faith is needed to cross the waters of death. A further possible indication of symbolism is hinted at in John's version when he states that, after Jesus got into the boat, they *immediately* reached their destination. Could this refer to immediate salvation? On the other hand, it could simply mean that the disciples were tired and confused after being in the boat all night, and that they were so near the shore that Jesus could wade out in the shallows or on a sand bar to reach them or, as suggested by Montefiore (2005)[3], it was just that the surf was high.

Both Ropes (1910)[4] and Blomberg (1984)[5] doubt that events such as walking on water took place exactly as described; they have either been transformed in the telling or their symbolic character precludes objections to their historicity. Blackburn (1992)[6] also comments that the evidence for nature miracles is not very persuasive, but that Jesus wanted people to believe in him: "happy are those who have no doubts about me" (Matt 11:4–6; Luke 7:22–23, GNB).

Verdict: There seems to be little support for a genuine supernatural event here where the laws of nature were over-ridden, although this cannot be completely ruled out for this or any of the Gospel miracles. Whilst there may be an obvious simple explanation, such as that the boat was in the shallows, there are obvious pointers toward a symbolic meaning concerning metaphorically sinking because of a loss of faith, and the need to call out to Jesus for salvation.

2. *Walking on the Water,* 60–66.

3. *Walking on the Galilean Lake,* 87–92.

4. *Some aspects of New Testament Miracles,* 482–99.

5. *New Testament Miracles and Higher Criticism: Climbing the Slippery Slope,* 425–38.

6. *Miracles and Miracle Stories,* 549–60.

Feeding the four thousand

Two Gospel writers report this event. Matthew (15:32–39) states that Jesus went up a mountain and was followed by a large crowd. Jesus said to his disciples that the people had not eaten for three days. When the disciples asked him where they could get enough bread in the desert, Jesus asked them how much bread they had. They replied that there were seven loaves and a few small fish. Jesus took them, gave thanks, broke them, and gave them to the disciples to distribute. They all ate their fill, and seven baskets of pieces were left over. The crowd was estimated at about four thousand men plus women and children. Mark's (8:1–13) version is very similar, except that the loaves and fish are dealt with separately, and that the crowd numbered about four thousand in total.

The GNB closely parallels the NIV but adds that Jesus gave thanks "to God" (Matthew and Mark), and substitutes "gave thanks" for the fish rather than "blessed them" (Mark). In the NKJV "wilderness" is substituted for "desert" and "multitudes" for "crowds" but otherwise it parallels the NIV account. There are no anomalies in the Greek version: *erēmia* means uninhabited place or desert; *ochlon* means crowd or multitude; *eucharistēsas* means gave thanks (Matthew); *eulogēsas* means gave thanks or bless (Mark). The GNB's addition of (gave thanks) "to God" thus may be implied but is not a literal rendition.

There are obvious similarities between this story and that of the feeding of the five thousand (vide supra)—the desert place, near the lake, the crowds of several thousand, the loaves and fish, and the baskets of fragments left over. Whilst only two Gospels report this latest feeding, compared with four for the previous one, there is still much detail that affords reasonable accuracy and reliability, assuming that they were indeed two separate events. It is possible that the passage of perhaps thirty years before the miracle was written down has led to the creation of the two versions of the same miracle. According to the Gospel accounts, however, many other events took place between the two feedings.

Matthew states that, after the five thousand incident, Jesus went across the lake to Gennesaret, did some teaching and healing there, then travelled to the land near Tyre (i.e. Phoenicia, about forty miles to the west) and Sidon (further north). Rather abruptly, the narrative then states "Jesus left there and went along by the lake" (15:29), climbed a hill and fed the four thousand. Mark concurs but adds that Jesus returned to Galilee via "the territory of the ten towns" (7:31), which would have included Damascus to the north, Scythopolis to the west and Philadelphia to the south. If these and the other towns were visited, the return journey would have covered well in excess of a hundred miles. Thus, chronologically at least, the two events are separated.

Trench (1850)[7] merely comments on the similarity of the two events, apart from the differences in the quantity of food at the beginning and the end. Montefiore (2005)[8] concurs but is more specific in suggesting there was probably a single source. Because most commentators do not single out this miracle for separate analysis, but combine the two examples for discussion, the reader is referred back to the earlier examination of the feeding of the five thousand.

Verdict: As with the previous case, this one has to be either a genuine supernatural event contravening the laws of nature, or the message is a symbolic one relating to spiritual feeding and a yearning for union with God. Alternatively, it was an exaggeration or there is a simple explanation such as that sufficient food had been brought by the people, or that the "meal" was a token one like the modern-day communion bread and wine.

---

7. *The Miraculous Feeding of Four Thousand*, 354–57.
8. *The Feeding of the Multitudes*, 77–86.

CHAPTER 16

VARIOUS OTHER NATURE MIRACLES

The coin in fish's mouth

ONLY MATTHEW (17:24–27) REPORTS this miracle. Whilst in Capernaum, the temple tax collectors asked Peter if Jesus pays the tax and he said "Yes". Shortly afterwards Jesus asked Peter from whom do earthly kings collect tax—from their own children or from others? Peter replied "From others". Jesus said that the children are exempt but, so as not to cause offence, Peter had to go to the lake, throw out a line, take the first fish he caught, open its mouth and in it he would find a coin. He then had to take it to the tax collectors on behalf of them both. The GNB wording is slightly different, including clarifying that "children or others" can be rendered as "citizens or foreigners", whereas the NKJV prefers "sons or strangers" and just refers to "money" in the fish's mouth rather than a coin. The Greek *uiōn autōn ē apo tōn allotriōn* is translated as sons or foreigners, whilst *statēra* is a silver coin worth four drachmas.

In addition to having a low reliability due to the single account and shortage of witnesses, this miracle is unique in that there is no confirmation that the prophesy was fulfilled—there is no mention of Peter doing what Jesus instructed. Some doubt, as does Montefiore (2005)[1], that this biblical report is accurate and few com-

1. *The Miraculous, the Mythical and the Paranormal*, 1–8.

mentators choose to include this example in their deliberations. Although Trench (1850)[2] discounts the simple interpretation that Peter was meant to catch a fish and sell it to raise the money for the tax, Blomberg (1984) does regard this as a possible metaphorical explanation or, alternatively, that one should just trust the Father to provide. Without attempting a specific explanation, Wright (1927)[3] regards this event as another example of the revelation of Jesus in nature and upon the organic world.

Verdict: In view of the low reliability of this report and the lack of confirmation that Jesus' prediction that a coin would be found proved correct, the most likely explanation is that the story was meant to be taken allegorically, for example that faith would ensure that God would provide.

Withering of the fig tree

There are two reports of this miracle. Matthew (21:18–22) states that Jesus was returning to Jerusalem from Bethany and he was hungry. There was a fig tree by the road but it was without fruit. Jesus said to the tree that no fruit would ever come from it again, and it immediately withered. The disciples questioned how this had happened at once, and Jesus replied that if they have faith and do not doubt, then they can do this to the tree and also move mountains. He concluded by saying that whatever they ask for in prayer with faith, they will receive. Mark's (11:12–14; 20–25) version is in two parts, separated by the pericope of Jesus overturning the tables in the temple (in Matthew, the latter precedes the full story of the fig tree). Mark adds that it was not the season for figs but Jesus still cursed the tree; it was only the next morning that the disciples saw that it had withered away. Jesus told the disciples that, whenever they pray they must forgive others so that the Father in heaven will also forgive them.

---

2. *The Stater in the Fish's Mouth*, 371–87.
3. *Miracles*, 186–91.

The GNB closely parallels the NIV, although it calls the "mountain" a "hill" and states that the tree was "dead" rather than "withered" (Mark). Whilst the NKJV follows more closely the wording of the NIV, an extra verse is included in Mark (11:26) which states that, if you do not forgive others when you pray, the Father will not forgive you. The Greek version does not have this extra verse, but the meanings of the key words are confirmed: *exēranthē* means dry out, or cause to wither; *parachrēma* means immediately, or at once; and *orei* means mountain or hill.

Whilst the reliability gains from having two accounts, Mark's is the more credible. Trench (1850)[4] notes that the story seems to attribute guilt to the tree for not bearing fruit, even though Mark's version states that it was not the appropriate season for it to do so. He hypothesizes that the tree might have been precocious and come into leaf prematurely, thus "boasting" but still without fruit, and was cursed for this. The story could be an allegorical reference to the sins of the Jews of Israel, who boasted but had little, whereas the other trees had nothing but did not pretend otherwise, as was the case with the Gentiles.

The idea of this story being a reference to Israel is supported by Blomberg (1984)[5] who cites other biblical texts with similar analogies, for example Micah (7:1–6) who likens Israel's moral corruption to trees where all the figs have been picked, and Jeremiah (8:13) who says that God wanted to gather his people but they are like a fig tree with no figs where even the leaves have withered. Guthrie (1970)[6] opines that this miracle could be a development of the story of the barren fig tree. This is told in Luke (13:6), and relates that the owner wanted to cut it down but the gardener asked for one more year to try to save it. Blomberg (ibid) suggests that this example, and Jesus cursing the fig tree, both depict the impending destruction of Israel.

4. *The Withering of the Fruitless Fig-tree*, 433–35.

5. *New Testament Miracles and Higher Criticism: Climbing the Slippery Slope*, 425–38.

6. *The Christian Imagination Theory* 193–202.

If, as Mark relates, it was not yet the season for bearing fruit, it seems rather strange that Jesus should curse the tree. An obvious or simple explanation could be that the tree was sick because it had leafed out of season and could not therefore survive (Trench, 1850)[7]. On the other hand, if this miracle has been faithfully reported, then it would further confirm the power of Jesus upon the organic world (Wright, 1927)[8]. However, as with the example of the coin and the fish, Montefiore (2005)[9] doubts the accuracy of this narrative.

Verdict: It would be a truly supernatural event if the tree withered instantly, but it is more credible to accept that it was not the fruiting season and that the withering occurred overnight because the tree was diseased. Taken literally, killing off a perfectly good tree would have been an untypically callous act, so an allegorical meaning relating to the destruction of Israel for its sins is a credible possibility.

Second miraculous catch of fish

This final miracle is the sole post-Resurrection example reported in the Gospels, and it appears only in John (21:4–11). After the death of Jesus, the disciples went out on the lake to fish but caught nothing all night. They saw an unidentified man on the shore who then called to them as "friends" and asked if they had caught anything. When they replied in the negative, the man told them to throw the net on the right side, and they then caught many fish. At this point they realized it was Jesus. Peter jumped from the boat whilst the others towed the net about a hundred meters to the shore. The net contained 153 fish but did not tear. Jesus had a fire and was cooking fish on it, and also had some bread. He asked them to bring some of the newly caught fish, and then distributed

---

7. *The Withering of the Fruitless Fig-tree*, 433–35.

8. *Miracles*, 186–91.

9. *The Miraculous, the Mythical and the Paranormal*, 1–8.

food to them. The disciples did not dare to ask him who he was, but they knew it was Jesus.

The GNB substitutes "young men" for "friends" when Jesus called out to the disciples, and the NKJV states "children". Whereas the NIV and NKJV record Jesus inviting the disciples for "breakfast", the GNB simply states "come and eat". Otherwise the three versions are substantially the same. The Greek version confirms "children" (*paidia*) in the NKJV, and "breakfast" (*aristēsate*) in the NIV and NKJV. Thus, again, the embellishments added by the GNB are not accurate in a literal sense.

The reliability of this report suffers by being restricted to a single account, but the author is named as one of those present in the boat. Although there are obvious similarities between this and the first miraculous catch of fish as recorded by Luke (vide supra), the two incidents were separated by many events, not least being the Crucifixion. Few commentators discuss this miracle independently of the first example, and Erickson's (1985)[10] comment relating to the earlier catch also apply here: that either the shoal of fish could have been seen from the shore, or that Jesus knew where the fish would congregate.

Trench (1850)[11], who commented on thirty-three of the miracles, regards this example as purely symbolic. He noted that there are subtle differences between the two "fish" miracles, such as the detail of how many "big fish" there were in the latest version, and the fact that the nets were not starting to break in the second instance as they were in the first. He regards the net breaking as symbolic of the schisms of the early church, and that not all souls were safely brought to land. Trench adds that now, after the Resurrection, there is a great "sea harvest of souls" but casting the net on the right indicates that only the good should be harvested. In the first example it was not specified where the net should be cast, so both the good and the bad were initially caught in the net. Jesus preparing the meal could be symbolic of the great festival awaiting in heaven, and the request for the disciples to bring their own fish could be an allegori-

10. *Providence and Miracles*, 406–10.
11. *The Second Miraculous Catch of Fishes*, 451–75.

cal reference to them bringing their souls to him. The mention that the disciples were tempted to ask Jesus to confirm who he was is intriguing: could his appearance have changed?

Verdict: This account contains many hints of an allegorical meaning, especially pertinent so near the close of Jesus' physical presence on earth, and was meaningful for the disciples who would need to continue their work as "fishers of men". Nevertheless, this final miracle should remain open to both simple and supernaturalistic explanations.

CHAPTER 17

SOME ALTERNATIVE EXPLANATIONS

THE ABOVE DISCUSSION AND verdicts on each of the thirty-five miracles was based on the pre-determined scheme where the default supernatural cause was challenged by alternative naturalistic, symbolic or obvious simple explanations. Whereas the healing, exorcism and raising-of-the-dead miracles were informed mainly by medical and psychological considerations, analysis of the nature examples drew on the views of other scholars. There are, however, some suggested explanations that did not fit this process and, for the sake of completeness, these will now be discussed.

The reader is also referred back to the earlier section of this report concerning the laws of nature, as explanations for many of the miracles depend on one's world view concerning these and, indeed, just what a miracle really is (Basinger, 2011)[1]. As Wright (1927)[2] opines, whilst some of the healing miracles might now be explainable with modern medical knowledge, they are no less divine for not being regarded as supernatural, nor are they precluded from being miracles (Twelftree, 2011)[3]. Although, as

1. *What is a miracle?*, 19–35.
2. *Miracles*, 186–91.
3. *Miracle in the Age of Diversity*, 1–15.

noted by Erickson (1985)[4], God cannot do the logically absurd such as squaring the circle or erasing the past, Wells (2010)[5] states that, if we consider only the currently accepted theories of physics, then the credibility of miracles would be improbable. Eichhorst (1968)[6] is not alone in suggesting that new or "higher" laws might one day be discovered that will explain some of the miraculous events.

Taken to the extreme, one possible explanation of miracles is that they simply did not occur. Guthrie (1970)[7], for example, voices the notion that they are dramatizations of the sayings of Jesus, such as those concerning healing the blind illustrating his bringing light into the world. A similar idea is voiced by Montefiore (2005)[8], who cites the view that the miraculous element does not belong to the original events but to later interpretations of them, whilst Blackburn (2011)[9] suggests that the nature miracles are either symbolic or were created by early Christians. Richards (1975)[10] restricts his analyses to the seven miracles cited by John, and his comments were included in the above analysis of the nature miracles. He notes that John fills his descriptions with symbolism and surrounds them with theological discourse. Richards adds that it is the meaning given to these by the Gospel writers that is important, and that it is misleading to try to distinguish between the natural and the supernatural.

In addition to the suggested explanations that have been incorporated into the present examination of the miracles, Montefiore (2005)[11] also offers explanations based on the paranormal. This approach departs from mainstream psychology and, by his own admission, has "lost the interest of most scientists." However,

4. *Attributes of Greatness*, 267–81.

5. *Miracles and the New Testament*, 43–59.

6. *The Gospel Miracles—Their Nature and Apologetic Value*, 12–23.

7. *The Christian Imagination Theory*, 193–202.

8. *The Miraculous, the Mythical and the Paranormal*, 3.

9. *The Miracles of Jesus in History*, 116–20.

10. *Taking the Miracles Seriously*, 27–29.

11. *Beyond the Natural order*, 12.

he suggests that Jesus had paranormal powers, and lists examples under four headings. First to be considered is telepathy, and Montefiore[12] believes that Jesus was able to know things that were happening at a distance, citing his knowledge of the death of Lazarus (John, 11:11–14) to which one could add the remote healings of the official's son (John 4:43–54) and the centurion's servant (Matt 8:5-13), plus the exorcism of the demon-possessed girl (Matt 15:21–28).

The second paranormal power is clairvoyance, the ability to see things not physically present, for which Montefiore[13] cites the miraculous catches of fish (Luke 5:1–11; John 21:4–11) and the remote healings. The third is precognition, the knowledge of events before they happen[14]. Although no miracles are specifically cited, this could be applied to most if not all of the miracles, as Jesus would have known what the outcomes of his actions would be when he performed them. Certainly the coin in the fish's mouth (Matt 17:24–27) would fall within this domain.

There are also no specific miracles linked to Montefiore's final paranormal phenomenon: luminosity[15], although this can be used to explain various visionary experiences and the transfiguration of Jesus (Matt 17:1–3). In addition to these, Montefiore[16] speculates that Jesus' post-resurrection appearances might have been "veridical hallucinations"—hallucinations corresponding to a real event such as the image of an absent person—which is seen by several people at once. He states that these are more likely to occur if the perceivers have an emotional tie to a deceased individual, and he adds that the biblical mentions of the resurrected Jesus performing physical acts such as eating may have been added later for apologetic reasons.

12. Ibid., 23–40.

13. Ibid., 41–50.

14. Ibid., 51–66.

15. Ibid., 67–76.

16. *Resurrection Appearances*, 105–14.

CHAPTER 18

CONCLUSIONS

THE DECLARED AIM OF this study was to examine each of the miracles of Jesus as reported in the four Gospels, with a view to seeing if the events could be explained rationally. This was undertaken with an open a mind as possible, and whilst trying to suppress the presuppositions that we all have. It certainly was not an attempt to argue that such events could not, or did not, occur, or to undermine the integrity of the biblical texts. For those with a passionate belief in biblical inerrancy, the conclusions from this exercise do not exclude the possibility that all the miracles occurred exactly as stated in the texts, and that all were supernatural acts of God with no account needing to be taken of physical constraints such as the laws of nature as we know them. In fact, taken overall, the conclusions would not provide useful support for a strongly liberal or skeptical view that miracles did not, and could not, occur.

To briefly reiterate what was stated earlier, the first task was to try and establish the most accurate rendering of the texts that describe the miracles. Toward this end, three English translations of the Bible were compared and a reliable version in the original Greek (Koine) language was consulted to clarify key words. The compilers of the different English texts drew from a range of codices and other ancient sources, none of which were the original versions, and each used their preferred phrasings for words and phrases, especially where there were uncertainties or ambiguities.

The analysis then turned to the more difficult task of trying to establish what actually happened at the time the event occurred. The reliability of the stories as we read them today is influenced by factors that include an approximate thirty-year delay before they were written down, and the numerous copyings, translations and editings that have occurred over the last two thousand years. Only two of the Gospel writers could have been direct eye-witnesses, and the variances in the parallel accounts sometimes suggest some rather blurred memories on the part of the writers or their sources. When an event is paralleled in two or more Gospels, and was seen by many witnesses, its reliability is enhanced. However, the lack of detail about the origin and duration of illnesses, as well as the long-term follow-up of cures, whilst understandable, detracts from the reliability of many of the healing miracles.

The Gospel writers, their sources and other witnesses, will also have been influenced by the situation that pertained at the time of the events (*Sitz im Leben*). The ancients saw God as the source of all activity, and would not have been particularly surprised by the wondrous happenings they saw. There was much expectation that the coming of a Messiah was imminent, and the people regarded miracles as legitimate acts when carried out by divinely appointed agents. For those who recognized Jesus as such an individual, there would have been a tendency to accept his healings and other works without the need for an investigation into just how they were carried out.

The belief that sin could cause illness, plus the lack of the medical and scientific knowledge we have today, would also lead people at that time to accept at face value events that appeared to defy explanation. Although the task of trying to establish the true facts is helped by a comparison of parallel accounts where these exist, the very fact that differences are often found can make an accurate understanding speculative, and it inhibits the process of rational analysis and explanation.

Once the best attempt to establish the accuracy and reliability of a miracle account had been accomplished, the philosophical-deductive procedure used in this study guided the process of investigating possible natural, allegorical or straight forward simple explanations. A conclusion that, for example, a miraculous cure can today be explained by medical or psychological knowledge does not detract in any way from Jesus using the laws of science or nature to perform a compassionate healing as and when he did so. In fact, to many readers, it might make the miracle more believable and meaningful than having to accept a cure that defies rational, scientific explanation. Likewise, an allegorical rather than a literal explanation, as favored by some of the early church fathers, can, like a parable, contribute a great deal of understanding to the message that Jesus was trying to convey (Blomberg, 1984)[1]. In the present study, some very meaningful examples of this were suggested for several of the nature miracles. In similar vein, due to the constraints of reporting and understanding, as outlined above, the suggestion that there may be an obvious simple explanation for a miracle need not cause doubt about the integrity of the biblical writers.

It is hoped that the present writer's attempt to obtain the most accurate version of what actually happened in the case of the thirty-five miracles, will help the reader to form his or her own effort to understand and explain them. Keeping in mind the constraints, reservations, and provisos inherent with this exercise, the summary below reflects the somewhat tentative and speculative present findings for the four main miracle categories.

(1) The healings

Accuracy and reliability

Of the seventeen reported healings, six are paralleled in three Gospels, one in two Gospels, and ten appear only in one Gospel. Based partly on this and also the amount of detail provided, nine are considered to have weak, five moderate, and three strong accuracy and reliability. The strongest evidence is for the cases of paralysis where a man is brought to Jesus on a bed, the healing of Peter's

---

1. *New Testament Miracles and Higher Criticism: Climbing the Slippery Slope*, 425–38.

mother-in law of fever, and the curing of the withered hand. Each of these miracles is paralleled in three Gospel accounts, have many witnesses and contain useful detail.

Explanations

The most likely explanation for nine miracles was naturalistic (including faith) healing, although a supernatural alternative was included for four of these and an allegorical alternative for another two. A supernatural intervention was the main conclusion for six events, with a naturalistic alternative for three and an allegorical alternative for one. An allegorical explanation with a supernatural alternative was suggested for one miracle, and in another case it was considered that no miraculous event had occurred. The two miracles for which only a supernatural explanation was suggested were the instant healings of a leper and of a man with dropsy.

(2) The Exorcisms

Accuracy and reliability

All but one of these six cases are paralleled in at least two Gospel accounts, and four were considered to have strong accuracy and reliability, with one moderate and one weak. The strongest evidence is for the case where demons were transferred to pigs, and an epileptic boy brought by his father, was cured.

Explanations

Each of these was considered to have naturalistic explanations, with one having a supernatural alternative and another having an alternative that no exorcism had taken place. The former concerns the remote healing of the demon-possessed daughter, and the latter the demon-possessed boy brought by his father.

(3) Raising the dead

Accuracy and reliability

There are three examples in this category, two being reported in just one Gospel and the third in all three Synoptic ones. Despite this, the detail of the events and number of witnesses resulted in a moderate or strong accuracy and reliability rating for all in this group.

Explanations

All three raisings were concluded to have had naturalistic explanations although one, the raising of Lazarus, had the alternatives of supernaturalistic or symbolic explanations.

(4) The nature miracles

Accuracy and reliability

Of the nine examples, one is uniquely cited in all four Gospels, with two appearing in three Gospels, another two in two Gospels, with the remaining four in just one Gospel. For reliability and accuracy, three were rated as strong, one as moderate and five as weak. The strongest, which were paralleled and contained useful detail, were the calming the storm, the feeding the five thousand, and Jesus walking on the water.

Explanations

Only one, the water into wine miracle, was considered to have a possible supernaturalistic explanation, but with simple or allegorical alternatives. A further two, the calming the storm and the first catch of fish, were regarded as naturalistic but with symbolic alternatives. The remaining six were regarded as most likely symbolic with all but one, the coin in the fish's mouth, having alternative simple or supernatural explanations. The symbolic examples comprise the two multiple feedings, Jesus walking on water, the second catch of fish and the withering fig tree.

In summary, the outcome from conducting the analyses through this procedure was that supernaturalistic explanations unequivocally survived the challenge by alternative naturalistic, symbolic or simple alternatives in just two cases: the instant healings of a leper and of a man with dropsy. However, the supernaturalistic premise was either the first or second alternative in another sixteen of the thirty-five miracles. The conclusion that a healing or exorcism was, or could have been, accomplished using what we know today about the laws of nature, medical science, or placebo cures does not, of course, exclude it from being a miracle enacted by a compassionate Jesus. Only where the conclusion was allegorical or symbolic, with no other alternatives, could there be serious doubt about a naturalistic explanation, and this occurred just three times in the present exercise: the healing of the invalid at Bethesda, Jesus walking on water, and the coin in the fish's mouth.

No amount of analysis or speculation can lead to an unequivocal explanation of miracles; it ultimately rests on a person's level of faith in the inerrancy or otherwise of the Scriptures. The present conclusion should thus be accepted as an honest and systematic attempt to try and understand what happened two thousand years ago. Conversely, the reader might choose to see these conclusions as heresy and reject them out of hand. As noted by Erickson (1985)[2], conservatives operate within a conservative world view, but liberals hold that there is no supernatural realm outside of the natural one: God is within nature, not outside it. Put another way, as did Blomberg (1984)[3], miracles act as signs for believers but repel unbelievers.

A suitable conclusion to this study might be that, whilst the testimony in the Gospels and the miraculous events in the life of Jesus do not constitute scientific proof; the evidence is sufficient

2. *Classical Liberalism*, 304–6.

3. *New Testament Miracles and Higher Criticism: Climbing the Slippery Slope*, 425–38.

to challenge the honest enquirer (Blackburn, 1992)[4]. Larmer's (2011)[5] view is even more specific when he states that, on scientific, philosophical, and theological grounds, belief in miracles is entirely rational.

Whilst these are the final thoughts on the present investigation, the reader's own conclusions might be informed by the many claims that miracles still occur today. Some of these are discussed in the following, final chapter.

4. *Miracles and Miracle Stories*, 549–60.
5. *The Meanings of Miracles*, 291–308.

CHAPTER 19

MODERN CLAIMS OF MIRACLES

Although the present aim of examining the miracles of Jesus, as recorded in the Gospels, is now complete, this concluding chapter looks at some of the claims that miracles similar to many of the biblical examples still occur. Mayhue (1994)[1] discusses the question of whether signs and miracles ceased with the original twelve apostles, as the cessationalists believe, or are still evident today—the noncessationalist position. The latter view is supported inter alia by the statement in James (5:14–15) "Is anyone among you ill? Let him call the elders of the church to pray over them . . . and the prayer offered in faith will make the ill person well".

This advice is no doubt an inspiration for those who practice healing today. For example, Peter Southern (2005)[2] is an American pastor engaged in the evangelistic healing ministry, and his little book is replete with many such examples, most of them performed by himself. His first anecdote concerns a woman who attended one of his services in Wales, weak with cancer. He commanded the cancer to leave her, she experienced a surge of divine power, and he then heard the woman say that she was healed. Apparently the local hospital confirmed there was no trace of the cancer, and the woman enjoyed many subsequent years of good health.

1. *Who Surprised Whom? The Holy Spirit or Jack Deere?*, 123–40.
2. *Jesus the Miracle Worker.*

Among his other stories are a witnessing of the deaf and dumb being instantly healed in Sierra Leone, his freeing of a child from pain who had been bitten by a scorpion in Calcutta, and a remote healing by himself and his congregation of a child in a coma in intensive care. Southern states that arguably the most amazing miracle he ever performed was broadcast on BBC2 television in 1975. X-rays had shown that a twenty-month-old boy needed reconstruction of a hip joint. The parents had written to him, and he had replied by sending them a faith-inspired letter and an anointed prayer cloth (see Acts 19:11–12 where items of cloth belonging to St Paul were said to have healed people). When the boy was asleep, the parents placed the cloth over the hip and prayed. They felt movement in the hip and found that new bone had been created, reconstructing the joint. He reports that this was later confirmed by X-rays.

Southern gives many more examples, including the healing of eczema, heart defects, the deaf, dumb, blind, and crippled but, with one or two exceptions, they are details of "instant" cures without pre- and post-medical corroboration or long-term follow-up. This must not, however, take away Rev. Southern's dedication to his healing ministry, and it leaves open the question of how much of his success can be explained by a placebo or faith effect, and how much is divine intervention through him.

Montefiore's (2005) suggestion that Jesus' miracles can be accounted for by his paranormal powers was discussed earlier in the chapter on alternative explanations. This includes that Jesus could tell what others were thinking through telepathy, which Montefiore[3] says is a *natural phenomenon* (italics added), and that Jesus could see what was happening elsewhere. However, Montefiore also notes that people claim to have such powers today, and that these can explain some contemporary miraculous events. He reports a modern instance concerning a government officer at a camp in Kenya, who was told by a local chief that a significant person who lived two hundred and fifty miles away had died. When the official asked the chief how he knew, the reply was "I see it".

3. *Awareness at a distance: Telepathy*, 23–40.

Seven days later a runner arrived with the news that the person had died at about the time the chief had indicated[4].

With regards to the paranormal category of precognition, Montefiore[5] cites a case from World War ll when a military driver stopped on a road fifty yards before where a bridge was supposed to be, believing that something was wrong. It transpired that the bridge had been blown up, and all in the vehicle would have perished had he not stopped.

Yet another example is biolocation, the gift of appearing and speaking to another in a different (remote) location. Montefiore[6] cites this as a possible explanation for the appearance of Jesus walking on the water. He also states that Padre Pio (1887 to 1968) could biolocate, as he had visited a hospital to heal a sick brother even though he had not been out of the monastery. With regard to resurrection appearances, Montefiore[7] describes two modern instances where people have had apparitions of friends or family members who had died, and he notes that phantasms of the dead appear only to people who have had emotional ties with them, as was the case with those who saw the resurrected Jesus.

Whilst making a general statement that there have been many remarkable cases of healing since Jesus' day, Montefiore[8] is prone to making uncorroborated statements such as that "the provision of material [e.g. food] from nowhere is a *well attested* paranormal phenomenon" (italics added). Whilst some of his reports of contemporary miracles might be genuine supernatural events, there is generally a lack of scientific rigor in his case studies, which leaves open the possibility of less miraculous explanations.

Keener (2011)[9] devotes several chapters of his two-volume detailed exposition of miracles to more recent instances from around the world. Commencing with blindness, he states that many reports

4. *Jesus sees into the Heart: Clairvoyance*, 41–2.

5. *Jesus' Foresight: Precognition*, 51–66.

6. *Walking on the Galilean Lake*, 87–92.

7. *Resurrection Appearances*, 105–14.

8. *The Feeding of the Multitudes*, 86.

9. *Healing of Blindness*, 510–23.

of cures date from the first part of the twentieth century and are thus now impossible to verify. Examples include a doctor reporting cataracts in a sixty-four-year-old woman being healed through prayer in 1916, and a twelve-year-old child from Newcastle-upon-Tyne, UK who was born blind having its sight restored by a pastor in 1927. Numerous similar examples from Africa, Asia and Latin America are given, but these are mostly second-hand or eye-witness reports devoid of detailed medical assessment both before and after the event. A more convincing example occurred more recently in the "West", where a medical doctor gave spiritual healing to a man who was incurably blind due to a destroyed optic nerve, and he was able to see again later that day.

Likewise Keener cites many examples of the healing of people who were crippled, such as of a woman in Cuba who was brought to a church service on a bed unable to walk but, after the congregation had prayed for her, she was able to do so. Another instance concerned a woman who had been paralyzed from the waist down being permanently healed during a church service. As with the blindness examples, medical evidence is rarely offered but, in one case, X-rays of the feet of a 12-year-old boy in Cuba showed that his bones had been malformed and crumbling. An evangelist and others prayed for the boy and, a week later, more X-rays confirmed that there was no more deformity in his feet.

When it comes to raising the dead, Keener[10] states that such claims are *fairly numerous* (italics added) today. Following the description of some ancient and medieval examples, he cites some early twentieth century cases such as a man in Massachusetts whose heartbeat could not be detected but, after some Pentecostals prayed for him, the man began to revive. Another case occurred in Memphis where a forty-two-year-old woman died of cancer and her body was placed in the mortuary. When a certain Bishop Mason prayed over the woman, she revived.

There are some medically attested examples of raisings, including the case of a pastor in Sri Lanka who died in hospital after a heart attack. After many attempts to revive him, the medics

10. *Raising the Dead*, 536–79.

finally gave up. There was an administrative delay in consigning the body to the mortuary, and people who did not know the pastor had died continued to pray for him. After twenty-four hours, the man revived and was found to have no brain damage. Another well-corroborated instance occurred in a hospital in Florida in 2006. A fifty-three-year old man died of a heart attack and the medics used all the modern procedures over a forty-minute period to try and revive him. A Cardiologist, Dr Crandall, certified the death and returned to his scheduled patients. However, soon afterwards, Crandall felt a compulsion to return and pray over the man, who by then was being prepared for the mortuary. After the doctor had finished praying, the man's heart restarted and he revived with no brain damage.

Keener[11] concludes with a fairly short consideration of non-biblical nature miracles. He states that walking on water is not a uniquely Christian idea, and that there are numerous ancient Indian stories of this ability. Also, early Jewish sources claim that storms can be stilled through acts of repentance. More recently, an Indonesian ministry team who hired a boat was confronted by a dangerous storm. After they prayed to God, the sea grew calm and this outcome had the spin-off effect of converting the Muslim boat owner to Christianity. Keener makes passing reference to other instances such as food being multiplied and even water being turned into wine.

Apart from the more limited nature examples, Keener's reports of non-biblical miracles are encyclopedic. Whilst his presumed aim was to include every known example from ancient to modern times is commendable, many accounts are very basic second-hand reports such as "a chronic bladder infection was healed" and "a person near death was completely and instantaneously healed through prayer."[12] Far more meaningful are the ones where he has personally interviewed witnesses and, even more so, are the relatively few with authoritative medical testimony such as those cited earlier. Whilst explanations for the apparently convincing cases,

11. *Nature Miracles*, 579–99.
12. *Supernatural Claims from the Recent West*, 499.

especially those concerning healing, exorcism, and the raising of the dead, can be offered on similar lines to those suggested in the present report on the biblical examples, a few defy such attempts and remain a source of mystery.

Final word

From this review of non-biblical, and especially the more contemporary examples of alleged miracles, notably the healing ones, it is reassuring to know that people of faith continue to turn to God in prayer in times of difficulty, and that on so many reported occasions their prayers appear to have been answered. Hvidt (2011)[13], in his consideration of patient belief in miraculous healing, however, reviews the situation from both positive and negative angles. With regard to the former, he states that faith in miracles helps patients find meaning and hope in situations where they would otherwise give up. By contrast, negative religious coping stems from the belief that God controls everything, including suffering, and can send accidents and punishments to individuals. Such a religious conviction may lead patients to reject medical treatments. Examples include the rejection of blood transfusions by Jehovah's Witnesses, or a preference for the power of faith over medical intervention by Christian Scientists, often with tragic consequences.

Thus, like many other aspects of life, each of us has to come to our own conclusion based on the evidence as we perceive it, our personal experiences, and our convictions. What is proof to one person may not be so to another but, as Hvidt observed, if God had not already intervened, as related in the Bible, we would have absolutely no knowledge of him.

13. *Patient Belief in Miraculous Healing: Positive and Negative Coping Resource?*, 309–29.

BIBLIOGRAPHY

Ader, Robert, and Nicholas Cohen, N. "Behaviorally Conditioned Immuno-suppression." *Psychosomatic Medicine* 37 (1975) 333–40.

Anonymous. "'Studies in Theology' and Hume's 'Essays on Miracles.'" *Bibliotheca Sacra* 071 (1914) 105–31.

Ardelt, Monika, and Cynthia S. Koenig, "The Role of Religion for Hospice Patients and Relatively Healthy Older Adults." *Research on Aging* 28 (2006) 184–205.

Barth, Karl. *Dogmatics in Outline.* London: SCM, 1949.

Basinger, David. "What is a Miracle?" In *The Cambridge Companion to Miracles,* edited by Graham H. Twelftree, 19–35. Cambridge: Cambridge University Press, 2011.

Bell, Brad E., and Elizabeth F. Loftus (1988). "Degree of Detail of Eyewitness Testimony and Mock Juror Judgments." *Journal of Applied Social Psychology* 18 (1988) 1171–92.

Blackburn, B. L. "Miracles and Miracle Stories." In: *Dictionary of Jesus and the Gospels,* edited by J. B. Green et al., 549-60. Downers Grove: IVP, 1992.

Blackburn, Barry L. "The Miracles of Jesus." In *The Cambridge Companion to Miracles,* edited by Graham H. Twelftree, 113-30. Cambridge: Cambridge University Press, 2011.

Blomberg, Craig L. "New Testament Miracles and Higher Criticism: Climbing up the Slippery Slope." *Journal of the Evangelical Theological Society* 27 (1984) 425–38.

Bray, Gerald. *Biblical Interpretation Past and Present.* Downers Grove: IVP, 1996.

Brown, Colin. "Issues in the History of the Debates on Miracles." In *The Cambridge Companion to Miracles,* edited by Graham H. Twelftree, 273–90. Cambridge: Cambridge University Press, 2011.

Butler, Trent C., ed. *Holman Concise Bible Dictionary.* Nashville: Holman Reference, 2001.

Cole, Alan. "Mark". In *New Bible Commentary,* edited by D. A. Carson et al., Nottingham: IVP, 2011.

Cousins, Norman. *Anatomy of an Illness— as Perceived by the Patient.* New York: Norton, 1979.

Deffinbaugh, Robert. L. "The Anticipation of Israel's Messiah." (June 2004) https://bible.org/article/anticipation-israels-messiah.

Douglas, J. D., ed. *The New Greek-English Interlinear New Testament.* Translated by Robert K. Brown and Philip W. Comfort. Carol Stream: Tyndale, 1990.

Eichhorst, William R. "The Gospel Miracles—Their nature and apologetic value." *Grace Journal* 09 (1968) 12–23.

Erickson, Millard J. *Christian Theology.* Grand Rapids: Baker, 1985.

Fairchild, M. (2014). *The Miracles of Jesus.* Study the Bible: (January 2014). http://christianity.about.com/od/biblefactsandlists/a/Miracles-Of-Jesus. htm

Friberg, Timothy, Barbara Friberg, and Neva F. Miller. *Analytical Lexicon of the Greek New Testament.* Crewe, UK: Trafford, 2005

Garland, Robert. G. "Miracles in the Greek and Roman World." In *The Cambridge Companion to Miracles,* edited by Graham H. Twelftree, 75–94. Cambridge: Cambridge University Press, 2011.

Grindheim, Sigurd. *Introducing Biblical Theology.* London: Bloomsbury, 2013.

Guthrie, Donald. *New Testament Introduction.* Ontario: IVP, 1970.

———. "John" In *New Bible Commentary,* edited by D. A. Carson et al., 1021-65. Nottingham, UK: IVP, 2011.

Hvidt, Niels C. "Patient Belief in Miraculous Healing: Positive or Negative Coping Resources?" In *The Cambridge Companion to Miracles,* edited by Graham H. Twelftree, 309–29. Cambridge: Cambridge University Press, 2011.

Holden, Robert. *Laughter is the Best Medicine.* London: HarperCollins, 1993.

Kaplan, Harold I., and Benjamin J. Sadock. *Modern Synopsis of Comprehensive Textbook of Psychiatry/lll.* Baltimore: Williams & Wilkins, 1981.

Keener, Craig S. *Miracles: The Credibility of the New Testament Accounts.* Vols 1 and 2. Grand Rapids: Baker, 2011.

Keith-Spiegel, Patricia. "Early Conceptions of Humor: Varieties and Issues." In *The Psychology of Humor,* edited by Jeffrey H. Goldstein, and Paul E. McGhee, 3–35. New York: Academic, 1972.

Kelly, Stewart E. "Miracle, Method, and Metaphysics: Philosophy and the Quest for the Historical Jesus." *Trinity Journal* 29 (2008) 45–66.

Koenig, Harald. G. *The Healing Power of Faith.* New York: Simon & Schuster, 2001.

———. "A Commentary: The role of Religion and Spirituality at the End of Life." *The Gerontologist* 42 (2002) 20–23.

Lally, Stephen. "Laugh your Stress Away." *Prevention, 43* (1991) 50–52.

Larmer, Robert A. "The Meanings of Miracles." In *The Cambridge Companion to Miracles,* edited by Graham H. Twelftree, 36–53. Cambridge: Cambridge University Press, 2011.

Larson, Mark J. "Three Centuries of Objections to Biblical Miracles". *Bibliotheca Sacra* 160 (2003) 72–102.

Lerner, Melvin J., and Dale T. Miller, D. T. "Just World Research and the Attribution Process: Looking Back and Ahead." *Psychological Bulletin* 85 (1978) 1030–51.

Levine, Michael P. "Philosophers on Miracles." In *The Cambridge Companion to Miracles*, edited by Graham H. Twelftree, 291–308. Cambridge: Cambridge University Press, 2011.

Lowis, Michael J. "A Novel Methodology to Study the Propensity to Appreciate Music." *Creativity Research Journal* 16 (2004) 105-11.

———. "Dreams and their Relation to Physical and Mental Well-being." *The Journal of Social, Political and Economic Issues* 35 (2010) 366–80.

Marshall, I. Howard. *Biblical Inspiration*. London: Hodder & Stoughton, 1982.

McKnight, Scot. *Interpreting the Synoptic Gospels*. Grand Rapids: Baker, 1988.

Mayhue, Richard L. "Who Surprised Whom? The Holy Spirit or Jack Deere?" *The Masters Seminary Journal* 5 (1994) 123-40.

Moberly, R. Walter. "Miracles in the Hebrew Bible." In *The Cambridge Companion to Miracles*, edited by Graham H. Twelftree, 57–74. Cambridge: Cambridge University Press, 2011.

Montefiore, Hugh. *The Miracles of Jesus*. London: Society for Promoting Christian Knowledge, 2005.

Morewedge, Cary K., and Michael I. Norton. "When Dreaming is Believing: The (Motivated) Interpretation of Dreams." *Journal of Personality and Social Psychology* 96 (2009) 249–64.

Morris, Leon. *Luke: An Introduction and Commentary*. Leicester, UK: IVP, 1999.

Moule, C. F. D. *The Gospel According to Mark*. Cambridge: University Press, 1978.

Nourkova, Veronika, Daniel M. Bernstein, and Elizabeth F. Loftus. "Altering Traumatic Memory." *Cognition and Emotion* 18 (2004) 575–85.

Novakovic, Lidija. "Miracles in the Second Temple and Early Rabbinic Judaism." In *The Cambridge Companion to Miracles*, edited by Graham H. Twelftree, 96–112. Cambridge: Cambridge University Press, 2011.

Olander, David E. "Signs, Miracles and Wonders." *Conservative Theological Journal* 10 (2006) 19–37.

Richards, Hubert J. *The Miracles of Jesus: What Really Happened?* London: Mowbray, 1975.

Ropes, James H. "Some Aspects of New Testament Miracles." *The Harvard Theological Review* 3 (1910) 482–99.

Seyle, Hans H. B. *The Stress of Life*. New York: McGraw-Hill, 1956.

Southern, Peter. *Jesus the Miracle Worker*. Chichester, UK: New Wine Press, 2004.

Speake, Jennifer, ed. *A Dictionary of Philosophy*. London: Pan, 1979.

Trench, Richard C. *Notes on the Miracles of Our Lord*. London: John W. Parker, 1850.

Twelftree, Graham H. "Miracle in an Age of Diversity." In *The Cambridge Companion to Miracles*, edited by Graham H. Twelftree, 1–15. Cambridge: Cambridge University Press, 2011.

Van den Brink, Gijs. *Commentary on the Gospel of Matthew*. (1977). www.elim. nl/theologymatthew.html

Waller, John. "Dancing Plagues and Mass Hysteria." *The Psychologist* 22 (2009) 644–47.

Watson, Francis. "Enlightenment." In *A Dictionary of Biblical Interpretation*, edited by R. J. Coggins and J. L. Houlden, 191–94. London: SCM, 1990.

Wells, George A. "Miracles and the New Testament" *Think*, 9 (2010) 43–59.

Woods, Andy M. "The Purpose of Matthew's Gospel – Part 1." *Journal of Dispensational Theology* 11 (2007) 5–19.

Wright, T. H. "Miracles." In *A Dictionary of Christ and the Gospels*, Volume 2, edited by James Hastings, 186–91. Edinburgh: T & T Clark, 1927.

Printed in Great Britain
by Amazon

78542762R00072